Border to Border

Border to Border

HISTORIC QUILTS & QUILTMAKERS OF MONTANA

Annie Hanshew

With an introduction by Mary Murphy

Photography by

John Reddy & Doug O'looney

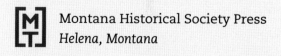

Montana Historical Society Press
Helena, Montana

Cover and book design by Diane Gleba Hall
Typeset in PMN Caecilia
Printed in China by C&C Offset Printing

Cover quilt: *Green Hills for Scottie*, designed and made by Shelly Van Haur,
photo by John Reddy
Softcover photo: Jessie Anderson and Ida Alnick embroidering in the front
room of a log house. Montana Historical Society Photograph Archives,
Helena, PAc 74-72.1
Frontispiece: Red and green floral quilt, Mary Y. Patterson, ca. 1847,
MHS 1989.82.01 (detail, appliquéd, 84" x 86", cotton)

This project has been partially funded through grants from Humanities
Montana, an affiliate of the National Endowment for the Humanities;
Montana Cultural and Aesthetic Trust; National Quilting Association, Inc.;
and Quilters' Art Guild of the Northern Rockies.

Humanities **MONTANA**   MONTANA CULTURAL TRUST
Partial funding for this project was provided by a Legislative Grant.   Quilters' Art Guild of the Northern Rockies

09 10 11 12 13 14   9 8 7 6 5 4 3 2 1

ISBN-13: 978-0-917298-64-6 (cloth)
ISBN-13: 978-0-9759196-2-0 (paper)

LIBRARY OF CONGRESS CATALOGING-IN-PUBLICATION DATA
Hanshew, Annie.
Border to border : historic quilts and quiltmakers of Montana /
Annie Hanshew ; introduction by Mary Murphy.
        p. cm.
Includes bibliographical references.
ISBN 978-0-917298-64-6 — ISBN 978-0-9759196-2-0 (pbk.) 1. Quilts—
Montana—History—19th century. 2. Quilts—Montana—History—20th
century. 3. Quiltmakers—Montana. I. Murphy, Mary, 1953– II. Title.

NK9112.H35 2008
746.4609786—dc22
2007042924

For Clara, who quilted some, and Louise,

who isn't a quilter but loves me just the same

Crazy, Ida May Brust, ca. 1900, MHQP 07-214-01 *(54" x 54", cotton, brocade)*

Contributors

MONTANA GUILDS AND QUILT GROUPS
Bits and Pieces Quilt Guild, *Dillon*
Bozeman Women's Activity Group Quilters, *Bozeman*
Falls Quilt Guild, *Great Falls*
Flathead Quilters' Guild, *Kalispell*
Miles City Centennial Quilters, *Miles City*
Missoula Quilters' Guild, *Missoula*
Peace by Piece Quilt Guild, *Livingston*
Quilters' Art Guild of the Northern Rockies
Undercover Gals, *Hardin*
Yellowstone Valley Quilters' Guild, *Billings*

PRIVATE CONTRIBUTORS
Lila B. Beck, *Great Falls*
Donna Demetriades, *Bozeman*
John and Brooke Flynn, Flynn Quilt Frame Co., *Billings*
Friends of the Montana Historical Society and
       Montana Quilt-Ornament Makers, Christmas 2008
Margo Krager, Reproduction Fabrics, *Bozeman*
John Lawton, *Great Falls*
LIATIS Foundation

Dr. Charles J. Marlen, *Great Falls*
Carolyn McCormick, Add-A-Quarter, *Franktown,*
       Colorado
Mary Mollander, *Great Falls*
Joyce Morgan, *Bozeman*
Katy Kellogg Nygard, *Gallatin Gateway*
Charlotte Orr, *Lewistown*
Pat Paynich, *Bozeman*
Jane Quinn, Quilting in the Country, *Bozeman*
Lee Rostad, *Martinsdale*
Penny Rubner, Penny's Gourmet to Go, *Great Falls*
Vicki Sherman, *Big Fork*
In memory of Leta Davis Sims, *Princeton, Kentucky,* and
       Xava Fisher, *San Juan Capistrano, California*
Pat Valente, *Bozeman*

GRANTS
Humanities Montana
Montana Cultural and Aesthetic Trust
National Quilting Association, Inc.

Sugar Loaf, quiltmaker unknown, ca. 1860–1890, MHQP 07-120-01 *(pieced, 63" x 77", cotton)*

Contents

Acknowledgments

IN rain and snow, hailstones and heat, women and some cooperative men came to help the Montana Historic Quilt Project document Montana's quilts at quilt days held around the state. In the November 2004 *Quilters Newsletter*, Shelly Zegart states, "It can safely be said that the quilt project movement is the largest grassroots phenomenon in the last half of the twentieth century." The Montana Historic Quilt Project, a committee of the Quilters' Art Guild of the Northern Rockies, has joined this movement, eventually recording and describing over two thousand quilts. This book is a result of Montana's effort. I would like to thank everyone who participated from the bottom of my heart.

I am especially grateful to Joyce Morgan, codirector and financial officer of the Montana Historic Quilt Project; to Margo Krager and Jane Quinn, consultants for the project; and to regional project coordinators Shirley Barrett of Kalispell, Elizabeth Marshall of Missoula, and Karen Stanton of Hardin.

—*Mary Law Mollander, Project Director,
Montana Historic Quilt Project*

Biscuit Puff, Melissa Howard-Jolley, ca. 1872, MHS 1986.139.01 (72" x 79", wool, silk, cotton)

The Montana Historic Quilt Project

IN 1971 the Whitney Museum of American Art in New York City mounted an exhibition of antique quilts titled "Abstract Design in American Quilts." The exhibit drew huge crowds and brought new attention to quilts as objects of art, and for quilt historians, it marked the beginning of a quilting renaissance. Although interest in quilting has ebbed and flowed, this most recent rebirth coincided with the feminist and counterculture movements, which emphasized greater respect for domestic work, folk art, and, especially, quilts.

Miles away from the New York art scene, Montana women never stopped quilting or cherishing old quilts, but this national resurgence of interest drew new attention to the state's quilting past and to quilts as both beautiful works of art and valuable historic documents. The effort to preserve the images and stories of Montana's quilts and quiltmakers began in Hardin in 1987 when Jackie Redding, Karen Stanton, and Sandy Weaver collected oral histories and registered 175 quilts in Big Horn County. Their findings impressed fellow quilters and motivated them to organize a statewide documentation project. By the fall of 1987, representatives from the seven Montana regions of the Quilters' Art Guild of the Northern Rockies had established a registration campaign, the Montana Historic Quilt Project. Each region held documentation days during which trained volunteers examined and registered quilts of all ages and conditions. Since the start of the project more than 2,000 quilts have been registered, and from April 2000 to February 2001, the best of the project's quilts were displayed in ten locations around Montana.

In the 1980s and 1990s, groups across the United States conducted similar state quilt registration projects, but these efforts differed in their scope. Some states, for example, did not document quilts made after the Great Depression. The Montana Historic Quilt Project was designed to be inclusive. Selecting the slogan "Territorial to Today" to describe the project's broad focus, volunteers registered even the newest quilts because one day those quilts too would be historic. Accordingly, this book does contain a short chapter on contemporary Montana quiltmakers, but it is by no means exhaustive. Montana is home to many nationally recognized quiltmakers and to include all of their amazing work would require several volumes.

To ensure proper preservation and wide access for researchers, the records of the Montana Historic Quilt Project are now housed at the Montana Historical Society in Helena. So that *Border to Border* might also serve as a research tool, each of the quilts included is identified by its MHQP number or, in the case of those owned by museums and historical societies which were not registered, by its catalog number. Although the registration days have ended, the Montana Historical Society continues to receive and process documentation for quilts from around the state, and anyone with a treasured quilt is encouraged to contact the Society's Research Center.

Border to Border is the culmination of the efforts of dozens of quilters dedicated to the preservation of Montana's quilt legacy. Through their efforts to gather information about these lovely folk art objects, these volunteers have made significant contributions to the

Joyce Morgan, codirector and financial officer of the Montana Historic Quilt Project

Karen Stanton (right) and Sandy Weaver record information about a quilt made by a member of Myrtle Hubley's mother's family in the Old Maid's Puzzle pattern during a Montana Historic Quilt Project registration day.

Mary Mollander, director of the Montana Historic Quilt Project, examines a Pennsylvania Dutch Rose quilt from the 1850s during a quilt documentation day in Great Falls.

study of history. We tend to think that historians spend all of their time researching in the archives, poring through boxes and boxes of dusty written records. But increasingly, scholars who study the past are looking at the things people *made* (often referred to as material culture). Folklorist Henry Glassie, one of the earliest proponents of the study of material culture, explains the value of including everyday objects in the investigation of the past: "Few people write. Everyone makes things. An exceptional minority has created the written record. The landscape is the product of the divine average."[1]

Quilts are extremely valuable historical artifacts because they traditionally have been made by women, a group that for a long time was overlooked by historians. While women left behind fewer written records than men, scholars can study quilts to trace changing cultural values, aesthetics, and technologies, thereby giving women their proper place in the story of America's past.

I appreciate quilts for the contributions they can make to our understanding of American history, but in the course of researching and writing this book, I came to love Montana's quilts not because of their larger cultural meanings but simply because they offer a starting point for telling surprising and poignant stories about individual Montanans. This book draws heavily on the excellent work of contemporary textile historians, but it does not pioneer new ground in quilt history. The reason is simple enough. In general, Montana's quilters (and the quilters who made quilts that traveled here) were not at the forefront of quilting trends; in fact, as the persistence of Crazy quilts well into the twentieth century suggests, they were sometimes very far behind the times. Neither did Montanans pioneer new patterns or techniques (with the notable exception of Northern Plains Indian Star quilts). Thus, the quilts in this book are for the most part typical of contemporary quilts

made by regular folks. However, ordinary Montanans did as much as the prominent ones to shape the history of the state, and their stories deserve greater recognition. Quilts made or brought here by everyday people tell the story of Montana in little snapshots: of births and deaths and moves and weddings and giveaways. They are stories writ small, stories that don't make their way into history books but are stitched into the seams of Dresden Plate, Grandmother's Flower Garden, and Crazy quilts.

More than anything, my connection to the women of my family inspired the writing of this book. My great-aunt Dorothy Wachob Lower makes beautiful quilts. On one visit to Dorothy's in Cleveland, Ohio, I climbed up to the attic to see her latest masterpiece, a vibrantly colored floral appliqué quilt. For someone whose needlework was limited to dabbling in cross-stitch, which I could do only because the holes were prepunched, the quilt was a monumental and wondrous achievement.

By contrast, Clara Wachob Hugus, Dorothy's sister and my maternal grandmother, produced what seemed to me, as a child, far plainer comforts. These thick patchwork jumbles, usually tied rather than quilted, were made solely for the use of her grandchildren who lived almost two thousand miles away in Montana. My brother and I burrowed under mounds of these blankets in the winter, but I did not at the time recognize how the warmth they provided was my grandmother's way of caring for us from afar.

I can remember two *quilted* items that my grandmother made. One was a small wall quilt in the shape of the United States that hung in the stairway leading to my grandparents' attic. The states were composed of very simple, somewhat cartographically inaccurate polyester patches. On the rectangle for Montana, she had embroidered four stick figures and a black dog—my

The Montana Historic Quilt Project registered more than 1,500 quilts by the spring of 1997. This example by Hattie and Bessie Preble is a pieced scrap quilt made in 1910 (MHQP 22-180-02). The quilt top is cotton and measures 88" x 90".

mother, father, brother, and me next to our German shepherd, Bert.

My baby blanket was her other quilt, an ivory whole cloth with embroidered animals on the front, fuzzy balloon-print backing, and satin ruffled binding. The embroidery has long since worn away, leaving only the outlines she drew, the binding is detached in several places, and the batting is spilling out where the fabric has disintegrated. But it is, by far, my most treasured possession.

I am not a quiltmaker, and although I aspire to develop the virtues of patience, artfulness, and exactness that quiltmaking represents, I cannot guarantee that I will ever make a quilt. Instead, I write this book as someone with a love for old things, a passion for Montana and its past, an enduring interest in women's stories and the artifacts that help us uncover them, and a connection to my grandmother I feel in a very real way when I pick up the quilt she made me.

—Annie Hanshew

INTRODUCTION

Remember Me—A History of Work and Beauty in Montana Quilts

BY MARY MURPHY

IN 1917 Amanda Freed came to Grass Range, Montana, bearing a quilt inscribed with the words "Remember Me." The phrase was not uncommon on traveling quilts, which often served as talismans from particular individuals or from a group of friends to a sojourner. But over the passage of time, as their origin stories have been lost, those inscriptions of love and friendship have absorbed different meanings. The phrases, as the quilts themselves, have become fragments, clues, tiny jeweled windows onto the experiences of women in our past. They hint at networks of kinship and friendship, of the disruption and promise of migration, of the love of things warm and beautiful.

We can mourn the fact that we know so little about Montana's historic quiltmakers, about what symbolic meanings they stitched into their fabrications of color and pattern. But we can also embrace their gift-giving spirit. Many quilts were gifts of particular significance for the original recipient—and they are also gifts from the past to the present. Historic quilts are invitations to contemplate the world of their makers, to wonder at the imagination and talent of past needleworkers, and to be inspired by a continuing tradition of artistry and generosity. They are ideograms of the private and public histories of this place.

The cutting of cloth and its reassembly into quilts has a long history. Most quilters today are careful to identify themselves; quilt labels provide titles, describe when and where the quilt was made, and sometimes include an interesting tale about its genesis. We are not always so fortunate with historic quilts. The phrase "anonymous was a woman," made famous by Mirra Bank's book about women's art, is particularly apt when applied to women's needlework. In the nineteenth and throughout most of the twentieth century, the predominantly male arbiters of what constituted art in America relegated quilting to "craft" and dismissed it as a domestic skill that served a function and was sometimes, almost accidentally, beautiful. It was not important to identify the designers and makers of such work. Certainly, thousands of utilitarian scrap quilts were made by women and worn out by their families, and neither their makers nor the people kept warm by them were concerned with having those quilts recognized as art. But quilt historians have charted a long parallel trail of quilts sewn of fine materials, with original designs, brilliant color combinations, and exquisite stitching, that are, by any criteria, works of art.[1]

Quilts are part of a wider legacy of women's needlework, and it is in that context that I offer this essay.

Modified Necktie, Mary Wells Gump, ca. 1920, MHS 1999.07.03 (detail, pieced, 56" x 62", cotton)

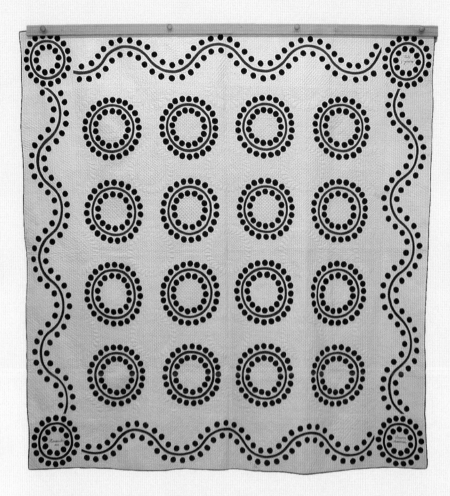

Remember Me *quilt, Susan Newcomer, 1872 (74" x 75", cotton)*

Necessity and pleasure are twined through the history of women's needlework. Before the advent of mass production of household goods and clothing, it was a woman's task to produce linens and clothes for her family, and the quantity and quality depended upon her family's wealth and her skill. Girls learned "plain" and "fancy" sewing, and many cultures prescribed the linens a girl should stitch before she wed. For many women, sewing of any kind was a chore; for others, needlework was a pleasure. Judged by the level of skill, design, and preservation, the quilts described here were the products of women who enjoyed working with cloth and color and who prided themselves on their stitchery.

Quilts are bearers of remembrance, often produced or presented in order to commemorate significant rites of passage in people's lives: births, christenings, graduations, engagements, marriages, anniversaries, departures, illnesses, bereavements, and deaths. They become palpable reminders of events that are frequently blurred interludes of joy or grief. Laura Heine's father died when she was four. In Heine's book, *Color Fusion*, the contemporary Montana quilter notes that the most

devastating legacy of her father's death was that he left nothing behind, "no letter, no tangible article that I could grasp onto, something left especially for me." She determined that she would leave "a trail that my children could follow. They will know me and remember what I did." Her quilts form that trail.[2]

A single quilt can carry in it a long history. Amanda Freed's *Remember Me* quilt, which is embroidered with the date March 1, 1872, arrived in Grass Range, already having traveled far. Born in 1852, Amanda Adams was apprenticed at age twelve to seamstress Susan Newcomer in the village of Wilmot, Ohio. Susan stitched the striking red-on-white appliqué quilt and gave it to Amanda, perhaps in 1872. Amanda had the quilt when she wed farmer Alex Freed in 1881. After he died, the quilt traveled with the widow and her son and two daughters to Wooster, where she ran a boardinghouse and put her children through the coeducational College of Wooster. Later, Amanda accompanied her daughter Hazel to Ann Arbor, Michigan, then to Denver, Colorado, and finally to Grass Range, Montana, where Hazel began a medical practice near the Winnett homestead of her older brother Elden and his family. *Remember Me* went along.

The quilt remained with Amanda and Hazel through the tumultuous years of World War I when Montana's homesteaders scrambled to meet the booming demand for grain, and the future looked bright. Hazel practiced medicine in the communities of Grass Range and Stanford for over forty years, traveling by handcar on the Milwaukee Railroad's tracks when winter roads became impassable, and rounded out her career as Judith Basin County's health officer. When Elden's wife died in the 1918 influenza pandemic, leaving

(top) *Susan Newcomer*
(bottom) *Amanda Adams (Freed)*

him a widower with two small children, Amanda and her quilt moved in. With Amanda caring for his children, Elden flourished, becoming, over time, Petroleum County's superintendent of schools, assessor, county manager, and a state legislator. When Amanda became ill, she returned to Grass Range, where she spent the rest of her life with Dr. Hazel, who inherited the *Remember Me* quilt when Amanda died in 1931. Hazel bequeathed the quilt to her sister Martha, who left it to her daughter Kathryn. As in the previous generation, sisters passed the quilt to each other, and Kathryn's sister Annabel Cornue Durnford finally donated it to the Museum of the Rockies in Bozeman. We know nothing more about the maker of *Remember Me*, Susan Newcomer, but quilters who visit the museum's collection marvel at the quilt's fluid design, her quarter-sized appliquéd circles, and her fine stitching. Her work, passed down through the hands of appreciative women, has left its mark. Susan Newcomer has not been forgotten.[3]

Every quilt has a story, although few are as well documented as Amanda's. To tell these stories, quilt historians have approached the study of quilts and quilters in a variety of ways. In many states, volunteer researchers have conducted quilt inventories, similar to the process that formed the basis for this book, in order to document the diversity of quilts, to identify their makers, and to ferret out the stories behind the quilts. Researchers also try to determine whether the quilts exhibited any regional or unique aesthetic and if experiences in a particular place might have been translated into a quilt's design. They also seek to explore how quilts have functioned as part of women's lives.

This book presents just a few of the thousands of historic quilts in Montana. In approximately ten years

of work, the Montana Historic Quilt Project has recorded more than two thousand quilts, and many historic quilts remain unregistered. Other quilts have been recognized as important to the history of Montana and have been collected by museums, most notably the Montana Historical Society Museum, which has more than one hundred quilts in its collection, and the Museum of the Rockies, which has ninety in its collection. In their permanent exhibits and in periodic quilt shows, smaller museums and historical societies across the state also preserve and display Montana's quilt heritage.

Quilts in Montana share a history with those in other western states. In her study of quilts on the Kansas frontier, historian Barbara Brackman identified a pattern in the survival of historic quilts in the West. Few surviving quilts were made in early-day Kansas; of the six quilts dated before 1880 in the Kansas quilt inventory, only one was made in Kansas rather than imported by early pioneers. Several factors accounted for this. Women were relatively scarce on the frontier and so was fabric—western states were not textile producers. Early female settlers probably carried bedding with them and had more pressing tasks to do than make quilts. The early quilts found in Kansas tended to be treasured ones transplanted along with immigrants—perhaps parting gifts from friends and family. As western territories became more settled and transportation networks extended further into the countryside, women began to have more time and resources to make finer, more elaborate quilts that were carefully tended and that survive today.[4]

Demographics are another important factor when considering historic quilts. Montana, until well into the twentieth century, was a white man's world. The first significant numbers of Euro-Americans came hunting gold

in the 1860s. Minerals, timber, livestock, and grain drew subsequent adventurers, speculators, and settlers—most of them men. In the nineteenth century, the Euro-American population of Montana was small—20,595 in 1870; 39,159 in 1880; 132,159 in 1890. In 1870 women were only 18.6 percent of the population of Montana Territory; by 1890, a year after Montana achieved statehood, women made up only 34 percent of the population. In 1910, soon after changes in homesteading laws made it easier to acquire land, the general population increased to 376,053 (a jump of over 54 percent from 1900). But women constituted only 40 percent of that number, and in the countryside, where the imbalance was greatest, there were 165.4 men for every 100 women.[5]

Across Montana, whether in cities and towns such as Butte, Anaconda, Great Falls, Billings, Miles City, and Fort Benton or on homesteads and ranches, women sewed. By the late nineteenth century, women everywhere in the state were accumulating the materials, tools, and skills to make clothing and household linens and then to turn their attention to more artful quilts. Because Euro-Americans settled Montana in the 1860s, many of the textiles, tools, and patterns that Montana women used for sewing were products of industry and commercialization, not home manufacture. In the first two decades of settlement, goods arrived by river and road. In 1860 the first steamboat that docked in Fort Benton

Montgomery Ward & Co.'s New Improved Singer Model Sewing Machine, With High Arm.

Price, $13.50.

28150 The above cut shows an exact representation of our new improved Singer Model Sewing Machine, *with high arm.* We handle one style only, No. 3, walnut drop leaf, box cover, and two drawers. Price, crated for shipment. Each.....................$13.50

Montgomery Ward and Company's 1895 catalog offered this Singer sewing machine.

carried troops and Indian annuity goods, but soon the boats were carrying goods for settlers as well. May Flanagan, who grew up in Fort Benton, recalled the "beautiful sight" of steamboats arriving "in the dusk of a summer evening with the glow of the furnaces showing thru open doors," and she loved the wonder of what might be unloaded. For her, a steamboat meant "new striped stockings or perhaps a new style hat, oranges and maybe grapes." Textiles were undoubtedly among the goods in these early cargoes. Dry-goods stores throughout the territory regularly carried bolts of cloth and sewing notions.[6]

Acquiring cloth was simplified with the spread of the railroad. In 1883 the Northern Pacific Railroad completed its mainline through southern Montana, and over the next thirty years the Great Northern Railway and the Milwaukee Road constructed transcontinental lines and branches throughout Montana, which facilitated the shipping of goods. Traveling salesmen, or agents, as they were often called, rode the rails to lure customers with all kinds of goods, including sewing machines.

Sewing machines became the first real consumer appliance. Elias Howe patented the first practical sewing machine in 1846, and subsequent improvements by John Bachelder and Isaac Singer led to its mass consumption. While patent infringement suits initially kept the sewing machine industry in turmoil, by the end of the 1850s the business had stabilized and rapidly expanded. Edward Clark, Isaac Singer's partner in the Singer Sewing Machine Company, pioneered

(right) Grace and Clark Mason after their wedding ceremony August 14, 1913, Kalamazoo County, Michigan

(far right) A page from Grace Mason's fall 1913 letter to "little sister"

consumer installment plans in 1856, enabling women to purchase a machine with as little as $5 down on a total cost of up to $125. A year later, he introduced the idea of allowing customers to trade in older machines for credit toward the purchase of a new machine. The industry exploded. As a result of extensive advertising, outlets in all major American cities, traveling salesmen, and monthly installment plans, five hundred thousand sewing machines operated in the United States by 1860. By 1900 the Singer Company alone was selling a half million machines per year.[7]

If a woman lived in a major Montana city such as Butte, she need only go to Hennessy's Department Store to buy her sewing machine. But anyone could order one through the mail, and, in fact, sewing machines were one of the most popular items sold by Sears, Roebuck and Company. Indeed, an early general manager for Sears, Roebuck claimed that "the mail order business was built to a great extent on the volume sales of the sewing machine." In the 1889 Sears catalog, five of its eight pages were dedicated to sewing machines. An innovative salesman, founder Richard Sears guaranteed every element of his machines: bobbin, shuttle, treadle, leather belt, cabinet, and varnish. He even guaranteed "that the neighbors would admire it." Montgomery Ward also prominently featured sewing machines, displaying its offerings in color on the catalog's back cover.[8]

Several innovations by the U.S. Postal Service, such as the initiation of RFD—rural free delivery—in 1898 and, in 1913, rural delivery of parcel post, facilitated mail orders. While freight charges initially made it pricier for western women to obtain sewing machines, the railroads' growth alleviated that. In 1907 a trade publication sympathized with the plight of sewing machine salesmen because their product "already has found its way into almost every home." By the early twentieth century, Montgomery Ward and Sears, Roebuck published twelve-hundred-page mail-order catalogs, known as "Big Books," allowing rural Montanans to familiarize themselves with the most up-to-date consumer goods.[9]

The experience of Grace Stoddard Mason illustrates the culture of sewing and its connection to consumer and transportation networks. Grace disembarked from a Great Northern train in Culbertson in 1913, a bride of sixteen days. The school board had hired her husband Clark as superintendent, and the couple arrived shortly before the fall school term. In a series of charming letters written during 1913 and 1914 to her family in Kalamazoo, Michigan, Grace described a young married woman's life in a small Montana town during the 1910s. Grace's days were punctuated with sewing. Among her new housekeeping goods were a blue quilt and rag rugs, and when a blizzard hit in September, another quilt hung in the doorway kept out the cold. Grace's mother had given her a dresser scarf before she left, and embroidering it and adding "Genevieve's lace" (presumably another relative) was "really something to keep busy at." She finished stitching it during a call from one of the town's ladies.[10]

Grace took great pleasure in dressmaking, frequently illustrating her letters with sketches of the clothes and hats she was constructing. By the time Grace arrived in Culbertson, the town had two clothing stores, a tailor, two milliners, and a notions store. Despite the availability of "store-bought clothes," many women, like Grace, sewed their own clothing, and like her, they purchased patterns from the *Ladies' Home Journal* and then shared them with relatives and friends, often altering and personalizing them to satisfy their own taste. Mail-order catalogs offered a wide selection of dressmaking materials. Grace confessed that one day she had the clothes sprinkled and ready to iron when a Montgomery Ward catalog arrived, and it so distracted her that it became "too late to get the ironing done before dinner time." While she might pore over the catalog, Grace was more than happy to send a traveling salesman on his way, impressing upon him "pretty forcibly that he might as well move on," for she preferred her own designs to the dresses he was pushing. In fact, she planned to finish a blue silk dress for the Halloween dance, noting that "all the teachers wear such 'foxy duds,' that I'll have to spruce up." Grace had her sister send fabric samples, piece goods, lace, and embroidery floss from Michigan because prices in Culbertson were so high. Eventually, Grace began sewing for other women and wrote home that she looked forward to starting a bank account "all for my own 'blowing,'" although deciding what to charge was at first a puzzle.[11]

While she sewed dresses and curtains, crocheted with the Ladies Aid Society, and embroidered with callers, Grace apparently did not make quilts. In a characteristically humorous letter to her grandmother, she wrote, "If you get out of a job and want a new one, I'll send money to get cloth to piece a small quilt for my first offspring. Haven't decided yet whether to have a boy or a girl. If I do decide on a boy I shall want the quilt blue, but Clark is fond of girls, so if I give up and let it be a girl, guess the quilt ought to be pink." Her grandmother did make a quilt, and although Grace would not have her first child until 1917, she wrote to her grandmother in April 1914, "I am glad to think if there really is anything doing, the next generation will be born with a quilt."[12]

As children, women like Grace learned all kinds of needlecraft from their mothers and grandmothers, and as adults those who enjoyed sewing, knitting, lace-making, and quilting could ply their craft and hone their skills in needlework groups and women's clubs. Montana women first formally organized sewing groups in auxiliaries to fraternal orders and church groups, such as St. John's Episcopal Sewing Guild, established in Butte in the 1880s. When the independent women's club movement emerged in the 1890s, sewing women had new opportunities to gather together. Some groups, like Butte's Marian White Arts and Crafts Club, were quite focused. Far more common were arts and crafts departments in general women's clubs, such as that of the Helena Woman's Club, founded in 1896. By 1926 the department hosted classes on rugs and quilting, tapestry, needlecraft, knitting, and cut lace. Members not only practiced various crafts but researched the crafts' histories and shared them with club members. At one meeting, four women presented "excellent papers" on hooked rugs, weaving, quilting, samplers, and tapestry. Two women scheduled to give papers failed to prepare them and had to pay "the usual fine" of one dollar each. At yet another session, Mrs. A. H. Tuttle gave "an instructive talk" on Ruth E. Finley's 1929 book, *Old Patchwork Quilts and the Women Who Made Them,* one of the first histories of American quilts. The club had more than forty members during the 1930s, and when they met in 1931 in the parlor of the YWCA building, "several pretty quilts were on exhibition."[13]

World, state, and county fairs and expositions were other venues that encouraged the display of quilts. For western territories and states, nineteenth-century fairs were primarily about abetting settlement. As early as 1874, in preparation for the Philadelphia Centennial Exposition, boosters argued that a Montana exhibit would "promote the interests of all our farmers, laborers, mechanics and tradesmen." The centerpiece

County champions at the Girls Sewing Contest of the Montana State Fair, Helena, 1913

of Montana's display at the World's Columbian Exposition in Chicago in 1893, for example, was a nine-foot-tall, solid silver statue of Justice, set on a plinth of gold. Exhibit planners, however, wanted to do more than simply demonstrate mineral wealth or the fecundity of Montana soil; they wanted to show that Montana would be a good place to call home. Thus, planners recruited women to furnish and decorate the state buildings at a succession of world's fairs and expositions and to exhibit, as the charge of the 1893 World's Columbian Exposition in Chicago read, "women's work, both usual and unusual."[14]

Montana women pulled out all the stops for the Columbian Exposition. Hand-painted china, fruit preserves, butter sculptures, and needlework were presumably counted "usual"; mineral samples from mines owned by women and a panoramic photograph of Butte constructed by "amateur lady photographers" were among the "unusual." The planners anticipated that "the needle work of the Gallatin County ladies and that of Lewis and Clarke will be equal to any there." While quilts may have appeared in state buildings as part of the furnishings, they were not a prominent feature at the Women's Building, which was devoted to American women's accomplishments. In one list of the building's 2,098 displayed items, only one bedspread and five "slumber quilts" were cataloged. All of them, interestingly, were from Montana. Unfortunately, we know nothing about them or their makers.[15]

By the twentieth century, state fairs had also become big business. In 1903, for instance, the Montana State Fair attracted twenty thousand paying visitors, and almost fifty thousand visitors came to Helena during fair week in 1914. Merchants knew that women fairgoers were an important clientele, and premium books often carried advertisements for local businesses that catered to their interests. In Helena the Raleigh & Clark Dry Goods Palace ballyhooed its fabrics and notions as well as Butterick's paper patterns and perfect fitting corsets.[16]

Sewing constituted a large part of women's fair work. The Montana Agricultural, Mineral and Mechanical Association held its first fair in Helena in 1870, and cash prizes were awarded for the best "worked quilt," "patch-work quilt," and "white quilt" in the needle-work section of Class VII, the "Ladies Department." The articles submitted had to be the exhibitor's handwork and had to be made in the territory. For the first few years, Class VII included sections for "needlework," "home manufactures," and "drawing, picture frames, engravings." By 1874 "home manufacture," which encompassed baked goods and preserves, had become its own separate class.[17]

Although other Ladies Department categories changed little between 1870 and 1880, needlework split into several sections, a separate one for quilts appearing in 1871. That year, the best silk quilt earned a set of solid silver teaspoons, and the best woolen and calico quilts won other silver cutlery. Judges first distinguished

Crazy, Ellen Busbee, ca. 1894, MHS *1984.28.01*
(73" x 85", satin, velveteen, brocade, taffeta)

between hand-sewing and "work done on machine" in 1881, awarding two dollars to the best specimen of quilting accomplished on a sewing machine. Thereafter, "machine work" became a regular section of the Ladies Department, separate from "quilts," which presumably were not quilted on a sewing machine. In 1890 a new category was created to accommodate the wildly popular silk Crazy quilts.[18]

In addition to the state fair, there were numerous regional and county fairs that celebrated the state's plentitude and possibilities; by 1890 their women's departments included such entries as the types of cut flowers, plants, and fruits that would grow in Montana. Boosterism extended to special categories of painting and photography depicting Montana scenery. Exhibits also pushed people to try new things: new crops, new plants, new arts and crafts projects. In 1874 the *Weekly Missoulian* extolled the potential virtues of a regional fair, claiming that as people gathered at exhibits they would be inspired to investigate and converse about the displays, picking up "all kinds of knowledge." The fair would instill "a spirit of improvement," including a desire to beautify and embellish homesteads. One analyst of the women's exhibit crowed, "[T]he women's department is a thing of joy and beauty to every feminine visitor. There they all can revel in old laces, embroidery and other garniture which appeals only to women." Quilts, presumably, were part of the "other garniture," and the

fair allowed quilters to study new patterns, fabrics, and exemplary workmanship. Historian Virginia Gunn speculates that "it is highly likely that these quilt exhibits helped shape regional taste and style preferences in quiltmaking."[19]

The changes in fairs' exhibit categories and premium lists give us an idea of how interest in quilting shifted over time and how quilting fit into women's lives. In her study of the Minnesota State Fair, Karal Ann Marling found that quilting declined in popularity after the turn of the century. Young urban women were presumably "'too busy with club work, with golf, and with automobiling to patch quilts.'" Instead, quilts came from the rural counties, stitched by women in their seventies, eighties, and nineties. A similar trend occurred in Montana. After 1900 the number of quilt categories at the Montana State Fair shrank. By 1905 there were no quilts in the girls' work division; increasingly quilt entries were relegated to the "Old Ladies' Department." In the 1910s quilts disappeared entirely for a couple of years and then new categories for appliqué quilts emerged in 1914. In 1915 the best cotton appliqué patchwork quilt earned a special premium of a case of Hiawatha-brand canned vegetables, worth five dollars, a substantial prize considering that most needlework premiums were one or two dollars. Over the course of the 1920s, however, quilt premiums were minimal, and in 1928 the Old Ladies' Department became "Aged Ladies' Work," which remained the chief venue for fair quilts until the state fair's demise during the Great Depression.[20]

Still, in 1933, when Sears, Roebuck and Company sponsored a national quilt contest in conjunction with the Century of Progress Exposition in Chicago to drum up fair attendance and business for the Sears catalog (which listed all the tools, fabric, batting, thread, patterns, and kits that a quilter might desire), the contest was a wild success. Approximately twenty-five thousand people submitted quilts, hoping to earn some of the $7,500 prize money, a vast sum during one of the darkest years of the Great Depression. The top thirty quilts, which were chosen at competitions that began at the local level and proceeded through ten regional semi-

Women's Missionary Society, Chippewa-Cree tribes, Rocky Boy's Reservation, Montana, 1930s

finals, were exhibited at the fair. Two Montana women won five-dollar awards: Mrs. Rosa Wells of Turner and Mrs. Jane Baker of Dell. In the 1990s, when Merikay Waldvogel and Barbara Brackman attempted to locate quilts submitted to the contest, they were able to identify only 123, including a Montana quilt made by Grace Skillestad. Undoubtedly, many other Montana women entered the contest; some of their quilts may yet come to light.[21]

Well into the twentieth century, sewing remained a key component of the pantheon of domestic skills, and sewing classes were staples of female education throughout the United States. In Montana the subject was generally taught in the last few grades of elementary school, most often in rural schools. Lessons such as "darning stockings brought from home; patching and sewing on buttons; lengthening skirts" also spoke of the frugality necessary on Montana farms and ranches.[22]

Sewing was also an important path to assimilation for Native American girls. Reservation schools, whether run by the government or missionaries, taught sewing as a practical skill. "Dressing white" was part of the assimilation process, and sewing would help prepare Indian girls for their future domestic roles as well as provide them with a marketable skill. As anthropologist Nancy Tucker noted, "[C]hanging clothing styles were an outward sign of hoped for internal changes and conversion." Mary A. Renville, wife of native pastor John B. Renville, a missionary in Dakota Territory in the 1870s, agreed with that idea, and she reported, as a partial success, children clothed in starched bonnets, white stockings, and moccasins. In 1908 a visitor to the annual Crow Fair, an agricultural exposition held on the Crow

Reservation, lauded the sewing and darning of Indian girls at St. Xavier Mission School. She singled out Josephine Pretty Medicine and Magdalene Horse Mane for their darning and complimented Pryor School student Lucy Plain Bull's "very pretty pincushion."[23]

Native women had, of course, sewn long before the advent of Euro-Americans, and when teachers introduced new tools, clothing styles, and techniques, Indian women grafted them onto their own aesthetics and skills. In 1876 Mary Renville recalled going into Indian women's homes to teach "making and quilting bed quilts and comfortables." White women's groups from various religious denominations shipped barrels of cloth for Indian women to sew and bought Indian women's beadwork, which missionaries sent back to home churches. In 1883 the *Iapi Oaye, The Word Carrier,* a newspaper printed in both Dakota and English, which began publication in 1871 "to aid in civilizing and christianizing the Dakota Indians, of whom over one thousand can now read," reported that the main activity of the women's society that year had been quilt making.[24]

Missionaries organized adult women's sewing groups, girls stitched patchwork in school, and individual Indian women also took up quilting. Mrs. Flora Chapin, a missionary working at Poplar Creek, Montana Territory, in 1885 reported that when "Lucy," an Indian woman whom she was training in domestic work, became ill, Chapin gave her quilt pieces to pass the time as "they seem to think them [quilts] splendid for warm weather, instead of their blankets." Another young girl to whom Chapin gave "cut-blocks enough for a whole quilt" and calico to set them together "went on her way rejoicing very much."[25]

Among the quilts draped over the upstairs railings in the Browning Public School gymnasium in this 1920s photograph of the Blackfeet Midwinter Fair are many with geometric patterns, including a sugan, Log Cabin, and Irish Chain.

During the Great Depression, government-sponsored sewing projects and home demonstration clubs kept quilting popular among Indian women. On the Fort Peck Reservation, James Garfield, an Assiniboine, and his wife Nora Garfield, a Hunkpapa Sioux, produced two remarkable pictorial quilts in the pastels so pervasive in the 1930s. The two virtually identical quilts, one bordered in green, one in lavender, present aspects of Assiniboine history and culture. James drew the pictures, and Nora embroidered them using stem, straight, satin, and seed stitches along with French knots.[26]

James's father James Garfield Sr., who was born in the 1860s and lived the way of life depicted by the quilts, related the information for each of the thirty blocks. Every block is numbered and has a central scene; twenty-two of them have additional embroidered symbols or figures in the block's corners. For example, in the center of block three, a woman slices meat for drying and in the four corners are a bear, deer, buffalo, and rabbit, the animals, as Garfield Sr. narrated, "who were the most abundant and provided the Indians with their meat." Many of the pictures illustrate women's work: smashing and boiling

buffalo bones to get grease, making pemmican, scraping and tanning buffalo hides, sewing moccasins, carrying wood. Blocks seventeen and eighteen illustrate the cooking of "fancier dishes," including turtle and puppy. The corners of block eighteen feature figures of a skunk, duck, gopher, and badger because they "were prepared in the same manner as the dog." While many blocks deal with hunting and food preparation, others chronicle play, ceremonies, and birth and death. Block thirty shows a newborn baby accompanied by a toadstool with healing properties, a slim slice of which was placed over the navel with the umbilical cord run through a hole in its center. The cord was then cut with a knife and tied with sinew; those tools are shown in another corner. The remaining two corners hold the baby's carrier and a cattail, the fuzzy head of which, when mashed, lines the carrier. Death is depicted in three blocks. Block twenty-two illustrates a warrior's burial. His body, wrapped in a buffalo robe, is placed on a platform in a tree, and his belongings are hung around him for his use in the next world. In the corners of the blocks are his weapons and shield. Another burial scene is conveyed in block

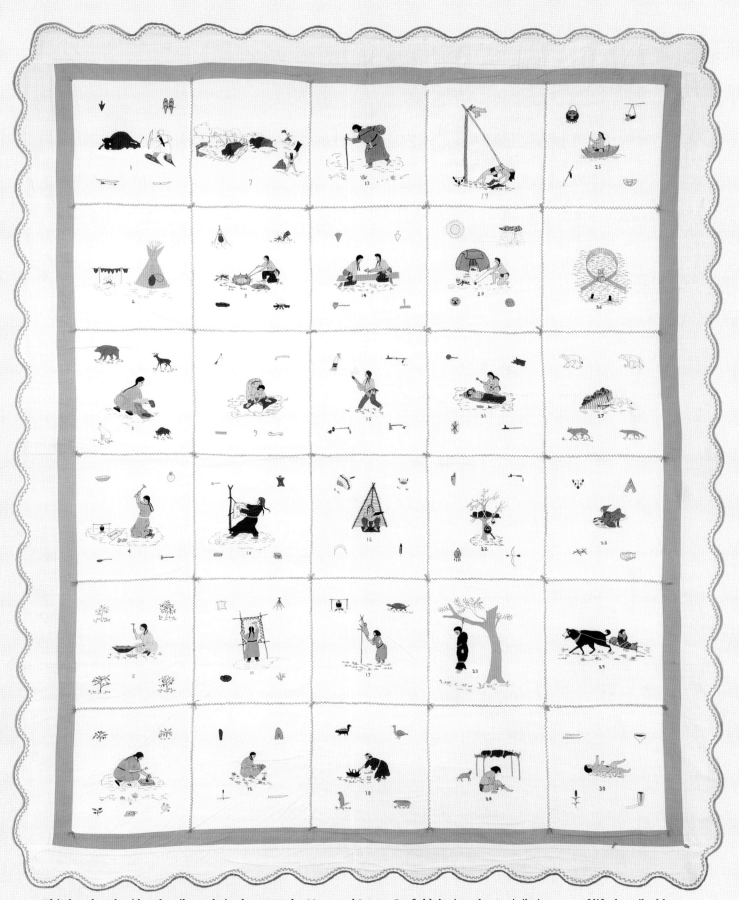

This hand-embroidered quilt made in the 1930s by Nora and James Garfield depicts the Assiniboine way of life described by James's father. Made of cotton, the quilt is 65" x 77".

The Star pattern that echoes the morning-star motif often painted on buffalo robes was the most popular quilt pattern among Northern Plains tribes. L. A. Huffman photographed one of the star-painted buffalo robes in this portrait of Hunkpapa Sioux scout Spotted Bear at Fort Keogh in 1879.

Morning Star, quiltmaker unknown, 1985, MHS 1985.92.01. This modern Star quilt was presented to the Montana Historical Society by the Fort Peck Tribal Archives in 1985 in memory of Sioux leader Gerald Red Elk and in honor of the Assiniboine and Sioux people. (Also see page 186.)

twenty-four, in which a robe-wrapped body lies on a raised platform and a relative with his braids cut off is slashing his arms and legs in grief. The most mysterious block is twenty-three, which shows an Indian woman hanged by her neck from a tree. In contrast to James Garfield Sr.'s other lengthy descriptions, here he writes only that "[t]his illustration pictures a squaw who has committed suicide." Unlike the other blocks, which render archetypal kinds of daily and seasonal work, this one apparently referred to a specific historical event.

These story quilts are unique. Indian women, for the most part, sewed patterns that were popular across the country. A photograph of the Blackfeet Midwinter Fair in the 1920s features the gymnasium at Browning draped with quilts more typical of the period; a sugan, Log Cabin, and Irish Chain are among the many geometric patterns. The Star was the most popular pattern among Northern Plains Indian women. For the Northern Plains people, quilts took the place of buffalo robes, which had often been painted with a morning-star motif. Some scholars say that Indian Star quilts echo the pattern of those painted robes, but no one has determined the exact origin of the design. Patricia Albers and Beatrice Medicine posit that Indian women probably borrowed the design from Euro-Americans who taught them to quilt and in that process "transposed the symbolism of the morning star from an old medium to a new one." Contemporary quilters also sometimes talk about the pattern as a representation of the sacred circle.[27]

Almira Jackson, one of the best-known Assiniboine Star quilters, posed with one of her Star quilts.

Almira Buffalo Bone Jackson, an internationally recognized Assiniboine Star quilter, recalled making her first quilt in 1935. Half a century later, she had lost track of how many she had made. Imaginative, as well as prolific, she once signed a letter, "your friend of raucous colors." Almira's quilts often began with a star in their center and then, spinning out from that heart, included other symbolic representations of her daily life and tribal culture. Quilts titled Night Time Sky, Deer Tracks, Star with Flying Arrows, The Story of the Assiniboine, Time to Make Dry Meat, and Arrows Shooting into the Star all employ the vivid colors favored by Assiniboine and Sioux quilters. Almira's quilts have been exhibited in museums across

Sugan, Lucille Meinecke, ca. 1930,
MHS 1987.19.05
(pieced, 70" x 85", wool)

While few diaries and memoirs mention quilting, mothers frequently wrote about scrabbling to get decent clothes for their children to wear to school. When Linnie White Greathouse's children wanted to go to Sunday school, she determined to fix them something to wear. For the girls, Arzetta and Odessa, she turned to her stash of one-hundred-pound flour sacks, and for her son Orley she took out a piece of yellow sateen she had been saving for a pillow slip: "First I sent to town and got dye. It was Turkish red, a beautiful color," she wrote in her memoir. "After taking the sacks from my pot of dye, I was really proud—not a streak or spot showed anywhere." She cut out dresses from the flour sacks and a shirt from the sateen. Her mother contributed white braid to trim the dresses, unusual black buttons for Orley's shirt, and the use of her sewing machine. Orley loved his bright yellow shirt, and, as Linnie recalled, "after the trimming of ruffles and braid, the little dresses looked pretty." Nonetheless, she advised her daughters not to tell people what they were made from.[30]

Among Euro-American Montanans, perhaps the most iconic quilt is the sugan, the heavy-duty wool quilt carried by cowboys, loggers, and sheepherders that had found its way north along the cattle trails. Described as "'hit and miss quilts' . . . because they just put them together anyway," sugans were durable and tough. On one occasion that toughness saved a Montana man's life. When rolling logs trapped logger Jim Flansburg in an accident near Evaro, his fellow workers rigged up a stretcher from poles, shoelaces, and a sugan and then hung it as a hammock in the rear of a Model T that was adapted into a log truck and trailer and used it to transport him to the hospital in Missoula.[31]

the United States and are in collections in Sweden, Switzerland, France, and Japan.[28]

Today, Star quilts are integral to Sioux and Assiniboine life. Women spend a good part of the year making quilts for giveaways at powwows and as gifts to mark births, marriages, puberty ceremonies, graduations, tribal elections, and the return of military veterans. Star quilts have roles in the sun dance, in the Lakota *yuwipi*—a nighttime curing ceremony—and in funeral rites. In the late twentieth century, Star quilt ceremonies became a fundamental part of eastern Montana basketball tournaments. Fort Peck families present Star quilts, often stitched with an appliquéd basketball, to opposing team members who have "displayed exceptional qualities of good sportsmanship."[29]

At the same time that women on Montana's Indian reservations were sewing, so were girls and women in Montana's non-Indian communities. Accounts of Montana homesteading are often tales of fierce poverty.

Heavy, durable wool quilts, sugans were usually made of simple plain blocks salvaged from old clothing. A glimpse of one is visible here on a bed in the lower left corner in the homestead shack of John (left) and Henry Haaven, East Coalridge Community, 1909.

The Treasure State may be the only place that can claim a poem inspired by the sugan. In 1940 John B. Ritch, cowboy poet and Montana Historical Society librarian, composed a ballad, "The Saga of the Soogon—The Ballad of the Sheepherder's Quilt," and dedicated it to his long-time friend Thomas O. Larson, a sheep rancher who had served in the Montana legislature and as president of the Montana Wool Growers Association. In the poem's preface, Ritch sets the scene—"Men's Social Room at the State Asylum for the Insane, Warm Springs, Montana"—and describes the narrator as "one of the sheepherder Inmates of the Asylum." Over the course of forty-two verses, Ritch blames the supposedly common insanity of sheepherders not on isolation, or coyotes' curdling cries, or the wail of winter, but squarely on the seams of the sugan.

> But 't was some bloodless fiend unknown,
> Whose calloused mind and heart of stone
>   Contrived a cursed quilt:
> A quilt made neither long nor wide,
> A quilt four-square on every side;
>   A thing so subtly built
> That men wot not its maddening plan,—
> Nor have they ever found that man
>   On whom to lay the guilt.
>
> A soogon quilt they called this curse.
>   What means that baleful name?
> What means soogon? Hell's pools immerse
>   His soul in tar-fed flame,—
> Nor no man knows, save him that wrought
>   This thing to cause our shame.

> Dire soogon quilt. Not long. Not wide.
> Too scant in length on every side.
>   To shield man's shivering form;
> Too scant to reach from chill-pierced feet
> To lend drawn shoulders needed heat
>   When winter's bell'wing storm
> Fair roars around his lonely tent,
> And all his sleepless night is spent
>   To hold his body warm.[32]

K. D. Swan, who joined the U.S. Forest Service in 1911 and was assigned to the Sioux National Forest with units in far southeastern Montana and western South Dakota, slept under a gamut of bed coverings as a guest of many ranch families. "A top covering of two or three sugans" on a straw mattress kept him warm, "even on a cold night after the bunkhouse fire had gone out." The occasional featherbed was a treat, and Swan, who grew up in Boston, admired the efforts women made to "bring to this frontier some of the tidiness and comfort familiar to her in some former home." He stayed in ranch houses furnished with family portraits and braided rugs, treasured pieces of furniture, and "priceless patchwork quilts."[33]

Some sugans have survived their hard use, but most historic quilts that remain in families or that are preserved in Montana's museums were special ones sewn to mark rites of passage or community or political events. In the late nineteenth century, the infatuation with Crazy quilts combined with the middle-class penchant for joining clubs and lodges enabled campaign and convention ribbons to make their way into many quilts. Now in the Montana Historical Society collection, Mary Kirby's 1893 Crazy quilt, pictured on page 78, incorpo-

This appliquéd quilt with fleur-de-lis design and Masonic symbols, possibly by Sophia W. Brown (1853, MHS 1999.56.187, 77" x 83", cotton) was made for Shelton Ransdell as a gift for his bride, Mary Elizabeth Brown, whose own Nine-Patch quilt is pictured on page 58.

rated political campaign ribbons to illustrate the battle over which city would become Montana's capital.

Women also stitched the symbols and ribbons of one of the most popular and influential fraternal organizations, the Masons, into a variety of quilts. Sarah Tracy, born in Illinois in 1851, traveled to Montana as an eighteen-year-old bride and settled in Bozeman. In 1896 Sarah made her daughter Edna a Crazy quilt, embroidered with Masonic symbols and an appliquéd Masonic ribbon from the 1892 state convention. Sarah Tracy knew the Masonic order well; in 1895 she was elected the Grand Matron of the Order of the Eastern Star of Montana, the Masonic Lodge women's auxiliary. In her journal she described the lodge as the place "within whose sacred precincts no feminine foot dare tread. Upon whose portals may be written 'Whoever enters here leaves wife behind.'" Graciously, she welcomed husbands to the women's group, "for with all your faults we love you still."[34]

In other cases, causes and events prompted clubs to work collectively on quilts, as gifts for members, as visual testimonies of belief and support, or as fundraisers. One of these quilts was presented in 1900 to Reverend Alice Barnes, the outgoing president of the Montana chapter of the Woman's Christian Temperance Union (WCTU), an organization that wedded American women's long-standing commitment to Christian welfare work with radical reforms.[35]

The Montana WCTU had gotten its start in 1883 when national president Frances E. Willard visited Montana to organize a state union; seven years later, Montana had nine local unions with over two hundred members. Prohibition was the WCTU's main cause, and each year it endorsed the Sunday closing of saloons and gambling halls and sought to convince churches to adopt the use of unfermented wine. The organization also supported a wide array of campaigns to improve conditions for women and children, including women's suffrage, improved wages for women workers, the placement of a police matron in the state penitentiary and in cities with populations of ten thousand or more, and better enforcement of juvenile court law.[36]

Approximately two hundred Montana WCTU members contributed silk ribbons embroidered with their autographs, and, in some cases, their communities' names to the quilt presented to Reverend Alice Barnes in recognition of her service. Many women embellished their signatures with small, blue forget-me-nots, the floral emblem adopted by the state union in 1889. Arranged in rows by community, the rectangles of ribbon are connected with white and yellow thread in a feather stitch and framed by silk strips lettered with the text, "For God and Home and Native Land/ Montana W.C.T.U./The Love of Christ Constraineth Us." The quilt is a fitting representation of the WCTU: it takes its form from traditional women's work, yet it is stitched with a roster of women who were committed to reform and who refused to remain anonymous. Today, Reverend Barnes's quilt, now in the collection of the Montana Historical Society, can be read as a text of Montana women's political and social activism, and their forget-me-nots as reminders of Montana women's work to improve the quality of life in the state.[37]

The United States' entry into World War I in April 1917 presented another opportunity for American women to contribute to the country's social welfare. Women's clubs endorsed an array of patriotic activities, including buying Liberty Bonds, signing pledges to conserve food, and, above all, working for the Red Cross.

Autograph ribbon quilt, For God and Home and Native Land/Montana, *Montana Woman's Christian Temperance Union,* 1902, MHS X1960.14.01 (49" x 60", satin, silk, cotton). In 1900 the Montana Woman's Christian Temperance Union made this quilt for their outgoing president Reverend Alice Barnes. About two hundred members contributed silk ribbons embroidered with their names and the state Union's floral emblem, the forget-me-not. Reverend Barnes is on the far right in this photograph of the Montana WCTU officers taken in 1900. The others are, from left, Mrs. I. N. Smith, Mrs. Matt W. Alderson, Mrs. W. E. Curran, Mrs. Anna A. Walker, and Mrs. Rose Ingersoll.

During World War I, women raised money for the war effort by embroidering the names of donors on Red Cross quilts and then raffling the quilts. This detail shows a section of names on the back of the 1918 quilt of the Ladies Auxiliary to Council 349 of the United Commercial Travelers, Cascade County (see page 102).

Popular magazines urged women to make quilts and "save the blankets for our boys over there." More common than quiltmaking, however, was sewing clothes for refugees and hospital goods for casualties; knitting sweaters, mufflers, and socks; and making bandages. Production of these goods was prodigious. Young women took up handiwork they had previously considered "work for grandmothers," ministers encouraged knitting during services, and the Red Cross kept meticulous records of the hours that men, women, and children devoted to needlecraft. Gertie Saunders of Billings, whose son Raymond was in the service and reported missing in action in October 1918, spent 2,969 hours sewing and knitting. By the end of the war, the Red Cross chapter of Yellowstone County alone churned out over 26,505 sewn pieces of clothing and hospital linens, 22,042 knitted garments, and 162,169 surgical dressings.[38]

In addition to figuring out ways to send bits of home comfort to soldiers far afield, Montana women also stitched Red Cross fund-raising quilts as a way of serving the war effort on the home front. Women appliquéd the organization's easily recognizable red cross on a white or off-white background in a variety of layouts and in exchange for contributions embroidered names of individual and organizational donors on the crosses and in the interstices. The finished quilts were then raffled to raise more money. Three Montana examples appear in this book. One of them, the Cascade County Red Cross quilt, initiated by Mrs. W. V. Roth and executed by the Ladies Auxiliary to Council 349, Order of the United Commercial Travelers (pictured on page 102), contains over a thousand names on its front and back. While some individuals chose to remain anonymous, appearing only as "a friend," most donors took the opportunity to proclaim their patriotism. Businesses, fraternal organizations, and labor unions—such as Great Falls Dairy Products, the Metal Trades Council, the Brotherhood of Railway Trainmen, the Scandinavian Fraternity, and the Sons of Hermann (a German fraternal order)—all paid

Red Cross volunteers gather at the Helena train station to greet arriving soldiers during World War I.

sufficient sums to have their names inscribed in prominent positions on this quilt.[39]

Another quilt that emerged from bloody conflict and spent a great many years in Montana originated with the Civil War. It represents the connections forged between the enormity of political and social events, the dailiness of women's sewing, and the sweetness of life stories. In summer 1864 the women of the Patriotic Society of Vernon, Connecticut, made several quilts for the U.S. Sanitary Commission, an organization founded to promote better field and hospital conditions for Union soldiers. Women, desirous of helping their sons and husbands, initially flooded the commission with clothing, bedding, and medical supplies and continued through long years of war to raise money and goods for soldiers' welfare. The commission encouraged women to form Soldiers' Relief Circles and requested that they make "quilts of cheap materials, about seven feet long by fifty

(right) U.S. Sanitary Commission quilt
(pieced, 50" x 80", cotton), young ladies
of the Patriotic Society of Vernon,
Connecticut, 1864

(above) Sanitary Commission stamp
on quilt back

inches wide"—quilts that would be useful for a cot, bedroll, or hospital bed. Northern women responded by stitching 250,000 quilts over the course of the war. One soldier described these quilts as "things of vertu."[40]

One quilt made by the Patriotic Society of Vernon and embroidered with the names of its makers was given to Captain Robert Emmett Fisk of the 132nd New York Volunteer Infantry. Fisk was born in Ohio but moved to New York in 1861, where he joined Abraham Lincoln's Republican Party and started a newspaper career before enlisting in the Union Army. In 1864 his unit was in North Carolina and, according to the story later told by his daughter, in dire need of quilts because Confederate troops had raided their camp and seized the majority of their bedding.[41]

Tucked into Fisk's quilt was a note from sixteen-year-old Fannie Chester with a list of the girls and women who had worked on it. Captain Fisk wrote to Fannie from "Oak Posts, Among the Pines, near New Berne, N.C." on September 18, 1864, to thank her and "her fair companions" and to assure them that their handiwork "has fallen into the hands of a soldier who is not altogether unworthy of your sympathy, your charity, and your prayers—one whose only mistress is his country and whose patriotism has been tested on many battle fields since the commencement of the war." Captain Fisk was a master of pretty prose, and having established the fact

that he was single, he clearly relished the chance to flirt with his quiltmakers, going on to praise the "sterling virtues of New England women: endowed, generally, with rarest gifts of face and form, and educated in head and heart to adorn the loftiest sphere of the sex." He was sure New England women made "the truest sweet hearts, the best wives, and most perfect mothers in the land." He hoped that Fannie would share his letter with the Society and wanted to assure them that having their names on the quilt meant that they would always be "warm in my remembrance."[42]

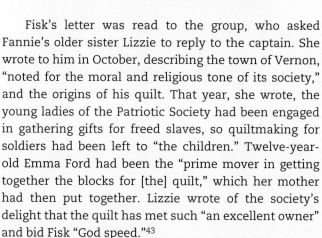

(far left) Captain Robert E. Fisk, 132nd New York Volunteer Infantry, ca. 1865

(left) Elizabeth "Lizzie" Chester Fisk, early 1890s

Fisk's letter was read to the group, who asked Fannie's older sister Lizzie to reply to the captain. She wrote to him in October, describing the town of Vernon, "noted for the moral and religious tone of its society," and the origins of his quilt. That year, she wrote, the young ladies of the Patriotic Society had been engaged in gathering gifts for freed slaves, so quiltmaking for soldiers had been left to "the children." Twelve-year-old Emma Ford had been the "prime mover in getting together the blocks for [the] quilt," which her mother had then put together. Lizzie wrote of the society's delight that the quilt has met such "an excellent owner" and bid Fisk "God speed."[43]

So began the correspondence between the Union captain and the self-described "Yankee school-ma'am" that continued throughout the war. The two exchanged photographs and increasingly flirtatious and intimate letters. Lizzie was relieved and delighted that by the spring of 1865 Robert had "passed safely through the contest." Robert planned to head west with his brother at the end of the war, but after his discharge in early July, he came to Vernon to propose to Lizzie. Lizzie accepted, but the wedding did not take place until 1867, once Robert had established himself and a Republican paper, the *Helena Herald*, in the recently created territory of Montana. They wed in Connecticut and then Robert escorted Lizzie and a new printing press by steamboat up

the Missouri River. Lizzie enjoyed her wedding trip. She watched the scenery, and especially the people, with a keen eye, penning vivid descriptions to her family back in Connecticut. Life on board the boat was entertaining; her company included gentlemen who played the violin and guitar in the evening and "industrious" and "lively" women with whom she spent the daylight hours, "sewing, knitting, reading, making tatting, & c."[44]

Lizzie's letters to her family, written between 1867 and 1893, chronicle the boisterous development of the city that became Montana's capital. Her intelligence and curiosity and her involvement in a variety of voluntary organizations, as well as Robert's position as a prominent Republican, fueled astute observations on the political development of the territory and state. Lizzie's acerbic wit make her letters a delight to read. In 1872 she was pleased to report to her mother that she had confronted a jeweler who had substituted inferior silver pieces for the ones the ladies had ordered as premiums for the Territorial Fair and compelled him to make good. As wife and mother of six children, domestic arrangements preoccupied Lizzie, and her letters are full of the tribulations and triumphs of housekeeping and motherhood. She kept her sewing machine in her dining room and continued to sew clothing, household linens, and at least some quilts throughout her life, including a crib cover that she quilted with red thread for her son Robbie.[45]

When Robert retired in 1902, the family moved to California. The autograph quilt that began Lizzie and Robert's courtship remained in the family and was donated by their descendants to the Lincoln Memorial Shrine in Redlands, California—one of a handful of surviving U.S. Sanitary Commission quilts. The quilt held great significance for the Fisk family. Lizzie and Robert's daughter Florence Fisk White wrote a short memoir about her parents' courtship, which concludes with Robert's return from Montana "to claim his bride of the Autograph Quilt." The quilt took on new meaning in 2004 when Don Beld of the Citrus Belt Quilters Guild of Redlands launched a project to sew quilts for

Above, bolts of fabric and rolls of quilt batting lie on shelves behind the dry-goods counter in Birney's general store in June 1939. The town of Birney is in southeastern Montana.

the families of local soldiers who had been killed in Iraq and Afghanistan. Beld, whose own quilts are often inspired by historical events, replicated the pattern of the Fisk quilt because he wished to carry forward the tradition of providing comfort that had been established by the Sanitary Commission quilts. Through word of mouth, stories in quilting magazines, and the Internet, the project expanded, first to the rest of California, then nationwide. By 2008 quilters across the country had made and distributed three thousand quilts under the auspices of what became known as the Home of the Brave Quilt Project.[46]

WHAT do quilts offer us in terms of understanding Montana's past? How should we evaluate the thousands of hours that the Montana Historic Quilt Project volunteers spent recording the sometimes comprehensive but more often spotty information they could gather about Montana's historic quilts? With gentle nudging,

or sometimes significant shoving, we can help people see quilts as art—as constructed objects of complicated design, color, and manufacture. But what do they tell us about Montana history, specifically about Montana women's history?

First, I cannot overemphasize the importance of the project's accomplishment in naming the makers of hundreds of Montana quilts. Anonymity has its uses, but when it erases the accomplishments of a significant portion of the population, it diminishes our understanding of who worked, who added comfort, and who added beauty to Montana's homes and communities. As we know, there simply were far fewer women than men in Montana during the nineteenth and early twentieth centuries, and they were not always readily visible. There were no shoe or textile factories employing hundreds of women, no large districts of boardinghouses to shelter single girls who came to the city looking for work and flooded the streets when their shifts were over. Domestic labor was, for the most part, interior, isolated work.

Log Cabin, Laura Harmon Howell, 1930s, MHQP 03-11-01 (pieced, 78" x 91", cotton)

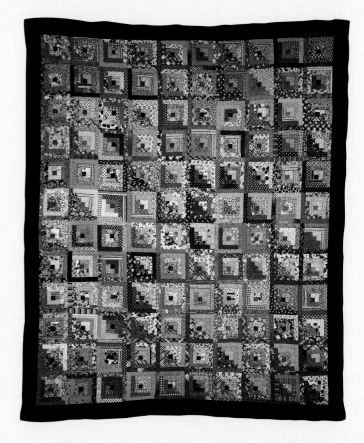

The community improvements undertaken by women's groups were easily overlooked. Not many casual observers would know that nearly every public library in Montana was originally the project of a women's club, that the flower beds outside county courthouses were maintained by local women's garden clubs, that the glass of milk drunk at a café's lunch counter was safe because women had lobbied the state legislature for pure food laws. In one very straightforward way, quilts are the vivid, tangible evidence of the work of thousands of Montana women.

Second, it is important to remember that the meaning of these historic quilts changes over time. In some cases, we know the story of why and how individual quilts were made, and even the reactions of those who received them as gifts, but, for the most part, what quiltmakers thought about their products and how they wanted the quilts to be viewed or used remain a mystery. Because quilts themselves are mute and subject to multiple interpretations, we need to distinguish between what they actually tell us about the past and what they mean to contemporary viewers. Historic quilts have acquired a romanticized, nostalgic patina, partly because our largely urban populace sees quilts as symbols of a bucolic rural past, in which handwork spoke of slower, quieter, perhaps more deliberate times. But I think we must resist sentimentality and overgeneralization when we look at historic quilts.

Certainly, many quilts made by Montana women reflect quiet moments and pride in handwork. In fact, many of them may indeed have been stitched in some of the only quiet moments hard-working women had. Considered individually, each quilt tells us something about a woman's skill and taste and, to a degree, her personal history. Taken collectively, however, these quilts reveal much about the social and political issues affecting women's lives. They demonstrate the ubiquitous sewing skills that women were expected to acquire, the charitable and political agendas of women's voluntary organizations, the pervasiveness of commercial patterns and fabrics, and Montana women's desire to share national fashion trends. If anything, these quilts demonstrate that women in a distant and overwhelmingly rural state wanted to be a part of the national culture.

Lastly, historic quilts give us an important medium with which to envision the past. When we study Montana's history, we can fall into the trap of visualizing a monochromatic place—most of the visual aids we have are black-and-white photographs. Yet when I look at historic quilts, I am struck by their color. I am impressed by the design and, frankly, intimidated by some of the stitchery. But I am dazzled by the colors. I think of a woman driving in a buckboard or a Model T across the grasslands of eastern Montana to discover that the new home her husband has built is a tar paper–covered shanty with a dirt floor, and I picture her hoarding her "pin money" to buy a bolt of Turkey red calico. I think of a woman in a four-square worker's cottage in Butte, looking out on an alley filled with refuse and laundry made grimy by the pall of smelter smoke and walking to Hennessy's after her husband's payday to buy a piece of fabric figured with brilliant chrome yellow and orange. I think of a woman in the Great Depression sweeping up the aftermath of a dust storm and sitting down for an hour to piece the cheerful pastel hexagons of a Grandmother's Flower Garden.

Quilts are compelling evidence that women created things of beauty in the midst of busy lives. Thinking about the choices of color each woman made when she pieced her quilt makes even the most anonymous figures of the past more human, more alive, more accessible to us. Imagination is the passport to the foreign country of the past, and quilts are among our most scenic pathways. ❖

CHAPTER ONE

Territorial Montana To 1889

*W*hen researchers for the Montana Historic Quilt Project put out the call for quilts, they received an astonishing number and variety made in the nineteenth century. Some were brought by pioneers who traveled to Montana in covered wagons, on steamboats, or, later, by train. Others were made elsewhere and inherited by Montanans in the twentieth century. Each of the quilts described in this chapter tells a story about Montana's development. The Sunburst quilt pieced by Nancy Ballinger, for example, came to Montana with her brother Merrill, who homesteaded in the Paradise Valley in 1880. Lydia Knox and Emeline Knox Morrison's Lily appliqué, an heirloom passed through the women of the family for six generations, arrived in Big Sandy with the homesteading family in 1913. The lush Crazy quilt shown at the chapter's end reveals the story of Pamelia Fergus, who arrived in Montana in 1864 and followed her husband James around the territory for sixteen years before they finally settled down on a ranch near Lewistown. She and her daughters began to stitch a quilt top while living in Helena around 1880.

Whig Rose (detail), "S.W.B." (probably Sophia W. Brown), 1857. See full quilt on page 24.

(left) Whig Rose, "S.W.B." (probably Sophia W. Brown), 1857, MHS 1999.56.185 (appliquéd, 86" x 88", cotton, wool, silk)

(below, top) Steamboat DeSmet at the Fort Benton levee, ca. 1870

In the lower photograph, the Whig Rose quiltmaker's daughter Mary Elizabeth Brown Ransdell Lord sits next to a bed made up with the quilt. Lord, in turn, gave it to her daughter Mary "Minnie" Shelton Ransdell Churchill, who brought it to Sun River in 1876.

Quilts are a fairly recent development in Montana's history. The area that would become Montana was a part of Louisiana Territory, purchased from France in 1803. A year later, Captains Meriwether Lewis and William Clark set out on a two-year exploration of the American Northwest, and they returned to St. Louis in 1806 with reports that the upper Missouri River was rich in beaver and otter. Almost immediately American and British fur traders flocked to western mountains and plains. Jesuit missionaries built the first permanent white settlement in Montana in the Bitterroot Valley in 1841. By the 1840s fur traders, too, had begun to establish permanent trading posts, including the one that became the town of Fort Benton on the Missouri River. That settlement developed into a trading center and steamboat port and served as Montana's link to the East.

The appearance of Euro-Americans initiated the displacement of Indians and the destruction of their rich cultures—the great tragedy of Montana history. By the mid-nineteenth century, Salish, Pend d'Oreille, Kootenai, Bannock, and Shoshone peoples lived in the western mountains, and Blackfeet, Crow, Gros Ventre, Assiniboine, and Sioux (and later Northern Cheyenne, Chippewa, Cree, and Métis) peoples lived in the eastern plains. Other Indian groups, while not living here, used the area as hunting grounds. Paradoxically, even as

Montana's first peoples were pushed onto reservations and forced to assimilate, one tool of acculturation—quilting—became for some Plains Indians a means to preserve their religious and cultural heritage.

Although fur traders and missionaries paved the way for white settlement in Montana in the early nineteenth century, gold sparked the first scramble to settle the area. The discovery of placer deposits at Grasshopper Creek in 1862 and a strike at Alder Gulch in 1863 set off the first major gold rush. By 1866 Montana had an estimated Euro-American population of twenty-eight thousand, and mining camps could be found throughout the western mountains.

Gros Ventre women sitting near tipis, 1908

These early Montana communities were transient and unsettled, as prospectors drifted from mining camp to mining camp in search of fortune. Because the frontier of the 1860s and 1870s was a rough-and-tumble place, it is sometimes easy to forget that many of these fortune hunters brought wives and families with them. Ella "Nellie" Gordon was one such woman. While making her living as a schoolteacher in the town of Cuba, New York, in the autumn of 1865, she met William "Billy" Asbury Fletcher, a widower with children who had just returned from Virginia City, Montana Territory. Nellie and Billy fell in love, and she nervously accepted his marriage proposal, even though she knew it meant moving to the Montana frontier. She wrote in her diary, "I could not help shrinking when I thought of going but I love him dearly & know that he loves me too."[1]

The Fletchers married in 1866 and, accompanied by several members of Billy's family, traveled by train and steamboat to Nebraska, where they joined a wagon train to Montana. The Fletchers' journey took them over the Bozeman Trail, a cutoff from the Oregon Trail that sliced through Sioux buffalo-hunting lands. In fact, because the Indian opposition was so great, Nellie's was one of the last of the immigrant trains to travel the road before it was closed by the federal government later that year.

Nellie kept a diary of her journey and wrote extensive letters home; her writings offer a woman's perspective of the overland journey. In a letter dated May 18, 1866, she detailed their wagon's sleeping arrangements: "I sleep as sweetly as at home. Our beds are very comfortable. I have a straw bed and feather bed and pillows,

Diarist Ellen "Nellie" Fletcher, 1866

one sheet and two blankets. Chell [Billy's sister] has the same, only no feather bed. Their beds, Chell's and Ella's [Billy's daughter], are in one part of the wagon, and Billy's and mine in the other. He puts boards across to fill out where the trunks don't come, and the beds are very comfortable."[2]

Although Nellie's diary and letters made no specific mention of quilts, historian Elaine Hedges notes that quilts could serve a variety of purposes on the overland trail, from padding china and protecting the exposed sides of wagons to burying the dead. Above all, quilts connected men and women to the family and friends they had left behind. Quilts brought from home were, Hedges observes, "visible and tactile reminders of connectedness, protests against the severance of ties but at the same time affirmations that physical distance would not destroy emotional bonds."[3]

Montana's gold rush slowed in the mid-1860s, but in the 1870s the territory found a new source of mineral wealth in silver. By the time Montana became a state in 1889, it produced nearly one-quarter of the nation's silver, and the communities of Butte, Helena, and Philipsburg had become the epicenters of its silver-mining industry. However, it was not silver but copper—discovered in late 1882 on the southeastern side of Butte Hill—that would shape the future of the state demographically, economically, and politically.

Although mining receives much of the attention in the history books, metals were not Montana's only draw. Cattle and sheep ranchers, who had trickled into the territory even before the gold rush, flocked to Montana's grassy eastern plains in the 1870s. In the 1880s the newly built Northern Pacific Railroad gave stockmen new access to distant markets. It was the heyday of the open-range cattle industry, a boom that came at the expense of the last of the buffalo herds, which were hunted to near extinction by the early 1880s, and Indians, who found themselves confined to smaller and smaller

James and Pamelia Fergus began ranching on Armells Creek in Fergus County during Montana's open-range boom. The bearded man second from left appears to be James; the others are unidentified. Also see Pamelia's quilt on page 66.

areas of land. Not until the frigid winter of 1886–1887, when nearly 60 percent of Montana's herds died, did ranchers learn the environmental limits of ranching on the Great Plains. But those with the financial resources and wherewithal to go on soon rebuilt their herds. Many of Montana's stockmen invested in sheep, which better weathered cold temperatures. By 1900 Montana was the top sheep-raising state, with six million head.

Although their presence in the history of the state is often overshadowed, the women who immigrated to Montana during its territorial days played an integral role in building young communities. Many westerners saw women as the civilizing agents of the rugged frontier. Cowboy Floyd Hardin summed up the respect felt for frontier women in his description of his mother and her peers: "There are no statues erected for, nor halls of fame dedicated to them, but they had a very big part in the taming of the West and making it a more safe place for the less experienced who were to follow them. We often hear of 'the forgotten man.' In my book, these pioneer women are 'the forgotten women.'"[4]

Many of the pioneer women who came to Montana brought with them an ideal of femininity that dictated how middle-class women should behave, what historians refer to as the "cult of domesticity." This ideology, whose tenets historian Barbara Welter identifies as "the four cardinal virtues—piety, purity, submissiveness and domesticity," first developed in eastern urban areas as a response to the drastic economic changes wrought by industrialization in the first

Jessie Anderson and Ida Alnick embroidering in the front room of a log house.

Thread advertisement,
ca. 1885–1895

time, skill, and money, served as one of the chief expressions of this type of domestic femininity.

The quilts described in this chapter reflect the evolution of quilting trends from the early 1800s to the late 1880s. In the early nineteenth century, generally only affluent women could afford the imported textiles required to make quilts. At the time, whole-cloth quilts were highly popular, in part because they emphasized tiny, meticulous stitching. Patchwork quilts, although not as common as whole-cloth, were also favored because using up small scraps of cloth underscored the industriousness and diligence of the quiltmaker and the individual blocks were portable and so could be more easily pieced.

Appliqué, the needlework technique in which a piece of cloth is sewn onto a larger one, also came into vogue around this time period. American women began to make appliquéd medallion quilts around 1750 using European chintzes and the *broderie perse* ("Persian embroidery") technique, which involved cutting the decorative elements out of the chintz then sewing them to a plain background. The medallion format featured large chintz cutouts at the center of the quilt, but quiltmakers occasionally added borders using appliqué designs cut from unprinted cotton fabric. According to quilt historian Barbara Brackman's *Encyclopedia of Applique,* the border elements moved from the periphery to the center stage around 1840; soon thereafter American quiltmakers abandoned *broderie perse* in favor of simpler designs and cleaner, repeated appliqué blocks. Conventional, block-style appliqué quilts remained fashionable through the Civil War.

Improvements in the manufacture of cloth made this change in appliqué fashions possible. As textile mills in the Northeast started to produce cheaper cotton fabric, women chose American calicoes over expensive European chintzes. More significantly, industrial developments made quilting accessible to more and more women. The availability of inexpensive fabrics, as well as other technological changes such as the invention of a pin-making machine in 1832, led to a "democratization" of quilting. For the first time, middle-class women

half of the nineteenth century.[5] Women were thought to be intellectually inferior and naturally submissive but also more pious and morally sensitive than men. A woman's place was in the home, where she could keep her family safe from the outside world, particularly those problems—crime, poverty, disease, materialism, and greed—that had come to the cities on the heels of industrialization.

Virtually no activity was perceived as more feminine than the creation of elaborate handwork, and thus sewing became an important symbol of womanliness. Historian Elaine Hedges explains how sewing came to define a woman's character: "By 1868, when Sarah Josepha Hale, editor of the influential *Godey's Lady's Book,* announced that not to sew was to be 'unfeminine,' the meaning of sewing had shifted: from being a useful, practical skill (which some boys also learned); it had become a way of socializing females into a narrowly defined and arbitrarily gendered notion of 'femininity.'"[6] Quilts, because they required enormous investments of

Double-sided quilt, Lucy Betts Goss, 1867–1889, MHQP 05-10-03 (58" x 82", cotton). The quilt patterns are Lemoyne Star (left) and Bowtie (right), both pieced patterns.

Laurel Leaves, quiltmaker unknown, 1840–1870, MHQP 36-03-02 (detail, appliquéd, 76" x 90", cotton)

could afford the supplies necessary to make quilts. This also meant that middle-class women could display the feminine virtues represented by quiltmaking, which had so recently been a pursuit of the well-to-do.

Although pieced and appliquéd block quilts were the norm through the Civil War, in the late 1870s American quilters suddenly broke away from the confines of block symmetry in favor of so-called "Crazy quilts." Made of silks, satins, and velvets and characterized by elabo-

rate embroidery and adornment, these frenetic-looking quilts were ubiquitous in the Victorian era. Many quilt historians trace the popularity of Crazy quilts to the 1876 Centennial Exposition in Philadelphia, where the Japanese pavilion drew massive crowds and inspired a fascination with asymmetrical art. Often used as decorative throws or wall hangings rather than bedding, Crazy quilts were, in fact, carefully planned and executed and painstakingly embroidered to display their makers' fine needlework skills.

The Montana Historic Quilt Project registration days uncovered a number of Crazy quilts, probably in part because these quilts were meant to be displayed and treasured and were, therefore, well preserved. However, most of the Crazy quilts featured in this book were made after statehood. Territorial Montanans, it would seem, were slow to embrace the Crazy quilt trend, perhaps because they were busy settling the frontier and needed practical, not decorative, bedding. Though not "crazy" in their design, the quilts Montanans preserved from the territorial period are still vibrant and elaborate, and they impress by their great variety and their luscious color. ✤

*Pineapple, Louise Parsons,
ca. 1880, MHQP 02-02-01
(appliquéd, 64" x 76", cotton)*

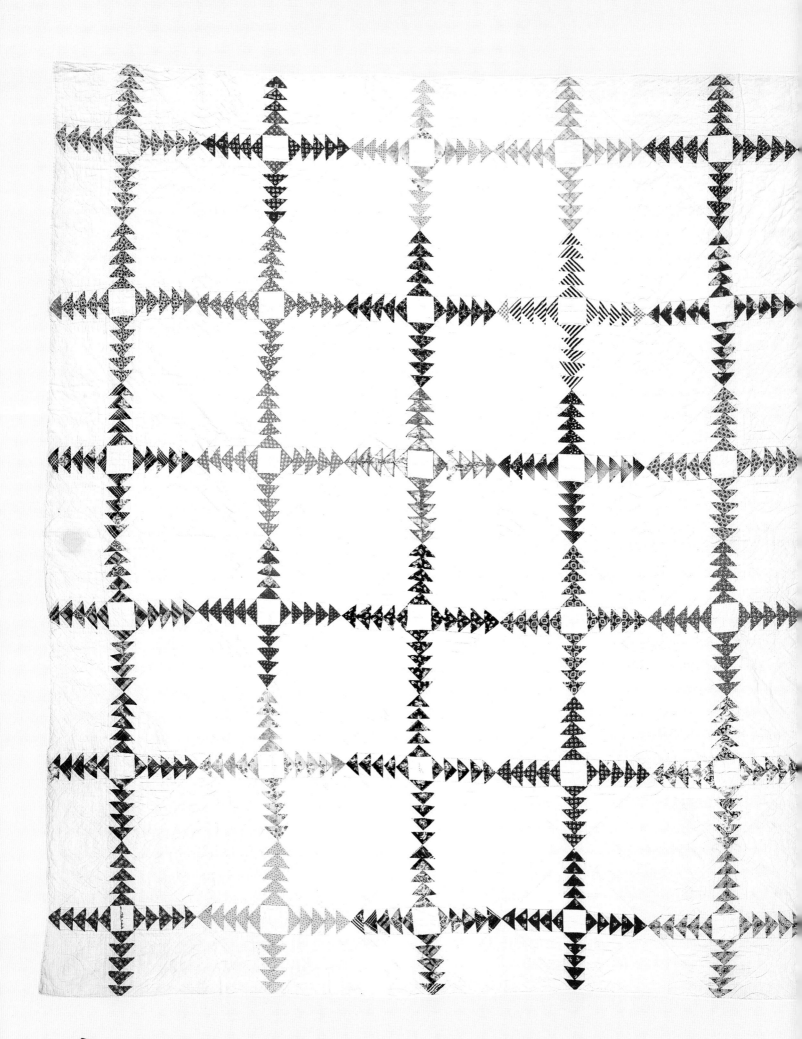

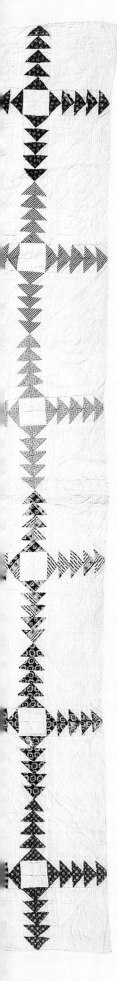

Goose in the Pond

QUILTMAKER UNKNOWN

early 1800s

ONE of the oldest pieces found by the Montana Historic Quilt Project researchers was this lovely and mysterious Goose in the Pond quilt. It traveled to Montana with owner Maxine Otis's parents, who homesteaded near Hobson in 1916, but additional details about the quilt are sparse. Researchers initially thought it was made between 1830 and 1850, but this theory conflicted with family tradition that had the quilt pieced in 1812.

Then the quilt began to tell its own stories. When researchers inspected its fabric more closely, it proved to be older than they originally thought, with some pieces dating to the late 1700s. They also discovered a date—1811—and a name—Robert McInnis—buried in the quilting.

Additional hints about the quilt popped out of the fabric. An ink inscription bearing the name Sarah H. Jones and the town Erie, Pennsylvania, was written in a corner block. Robert McInnis's name was also inked into the quilt, although the "c" and "I" in his name had faded.

We can only speculate about Robert and Sarah. Robert McInnis does not appear in the Pennsylvania census records. A Robert McGinnis farmed in northeastern Pennsylvania, and two of his neighbors in 1850 were George Jones and Harrison Jones, but neither had a Sarah in his household in that year. Whatever bond Robert and Sarah shared, the quilt was clearly a treasured possession. Reliable permanent ink was not available until the 1830s, so the inscription was probably added after the quilt was made and was intended to leave a lasting record of those connected to it.

"Sarah H. Jones, Erie, Pa."

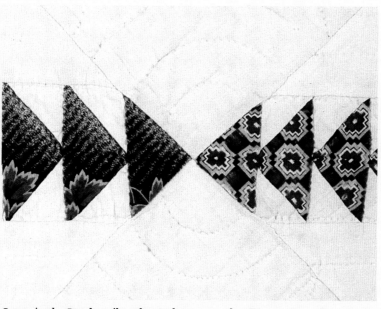

Goose in the Pond, quiltmaker unknown, early 1800s, MHQP 36-42-02
(77" x 78", cotton)

Sunburst

THIS Sunburst quilt was not made in Montana but traveled here, like so many quilts, with some of Montana's earliest pioneers. Nancy Ballinger, born to Kentucky homesteaders Henry and Lucy Jeffries Ballinger in 1814, began piecing this quilt in 1824, at the young age of nine or ten. She finished quilting it in 1832, the same year she married John H. Ballinger. The work is truly remarkable for someone so young. Jane Davidson Klockman of Bozeman, who now owns the family heirloom, guesses that Nancy's mother or one of her four sisters may have helped piece the quilt.

Nancy and John had two children, but she gifted her finished quilt to her youngest brother, Merrill. Five years Nancy's junior, Merrill moved several times: to Illinois, where he met and married Jane Hardcastle and the couple had eight children; and then to Missouri, where he worked as a farmer and druggist. In 1879, when Jane contracted tuberculosis and her doctors advised her to move to "high country," the Ballingers' eldest son Joseph traveled to Montana Territory to homestead in the Paradise Valley on the upper Yellowstone River.

The next year, Merrill brought the rest of the family to Montana by covered wagon along the Bozeman Trail. His three young daughters walked most of the way, as there was no extra room on the wagon. When the Ballingers passed the site of the Little Bighorn battle, the girls were drawn to a strange-looking structure: "[T]hey investigated it, as children would, and found a pen that contained some unburied bones from the Custer tragedy of four years before."[7] Jane does not know if her great-grandfather brought his sister's quilt with him during the 1880 overland wagon journey or if it was carried to Montana at a later date by family visiting from the Midwest.

According to quilt historian Barbara Brackman, this quilt pattern has at least six names: Sunburst, Kansas Sunflower, Noonday, Oklahoma Sunburst, Rising Sun, and Russian Sunflower, all evoking the radiance of the pattern. Nancy's version of the Sunburst is intriguing because the blocks contain fifteen-point circles instead of the typical sixteen, yet the circles are still incredibly uniform and precise.

Nancy gave her quilt to her youngest brother Merrill Smith Ballinger, pictured here ca. 1875.

Sunburst, Nancy B. Ballinger, ca. 1832, MHQP 06-130-05 (82" x 94", cotton)

Whole Cloth

REBECCA DRING &
REBECCA ROBINSON

ca. 1840

QUILTS are cherished heirlooms, in part because they connect women across distance and time to their mothers, grandmothers, aunts, and friends. When Mary Jane Lickiss immigrated from England to New Orleans in the 1850s, she brought this exquisite cotton whole-cloth quilt as a tangible reminder of two important women in her life. Mary Jane's maternal and paternal grandmothers, Rebecca Dring and Rebecca Robinson, made the quilt using fabric from their wedding dresses and petticoats around the time of their granddaughter's birth in 1840. Mary Jane married Elias Pickles in Steelville, Illinois, in 1859. As the quilt was passed down through the family, it continued its journey west and is now owned by Reva Parker of Bozeman, the great-great-great-great-granddaughter of Dring and Robinson.

This whole-cloth quilt was a unique discovery for the Montana Historic Quilt Project because it displays an old printing technique. Although most English textile manufacturers printed fabric using copper rollers by the 1840s, the cloth for this quilt was printed using an older woodblock method. This use of older technology makes sense, as the grandmothers' wedding dresses would have been much older than the quilt itself. To make a woodblock print, the printer carved a design in relief on a woodblock, and then the design was stamped onto the fabric. Each color on the fabric required a separate block, although occasionally extra colors were hand-painted.

While this is properly considered a whole-cloth quilt, the name is somewhat misleading because each section is actually made up of many pieces of material but pieced in a way that makes it look seamless. Look carefully and you will see that the quilt's center section, with a trailing vine motif, is composed of thirty-three separate pieces of material. The three-sided border, with its bouquet-in-a-floral-diamond print, is constructed from about twenty pieces. The grandmothers skillfully aligned the dress pieces to maintain the integrity of the woodblock prints, a technique that was common in the whole-cloth quilts.

*Whole Cloth, Rebecca Dring and Rebecca Robinson,
ca. 1840, MHQP 06-156-01 (90" x 98", cotton)*

True Lover's Knot

REBECCA MILLER

ca. 1850

REBECCA Miller used scherenschnitte, the German folk art of paper cutting, to create the intricate and bold appliqué pattern for this quilt. In the same way a child makes paper snowflakes at Christmastime, Rebecca cut out her intricate pattern on folded paper so the design would have symmetrical sides. Her cutout then became the pattern for her appliqué elements.

An ancient art traditionally practiced in many Asian and European cultures, paper cutting was brought to the United States by Swiss and German immigrants in the late eighteenth century. Scherenschnitte was popular throughout the nineteenth century, particularly among the Pennsylvania Dutch, who used it to make everything from Christmas ornaments to elaborately designed birth certificates. While many scherenschnitte artists used the same folding technique as Rebecca did, traditional scherenschnitte was frequently asymmetrical.

Rebecca Miller made this quilt in Indiana when she was twenty years old. She died two years later, shortly after giving birth to her daughter Mary Jane. However, her eye for composition and talent for quilting seems to be her family legacy, as Rebecca's granddaughter Hazel Wilder also became a talented and prolific quilter. Her Tulip quilt is included in Chapter 4.

Classical design from a 1815–1816 book about paper cutting

True Lover's Knot, Rebecca Miller, ca. 1850, MHQP 19-36-01 (73" x 85", cotton)

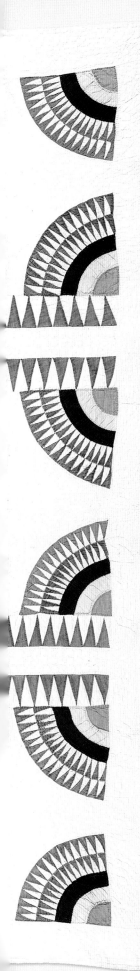

Railroad to the Rockies

RACHEL MUIR

mid-1800s

WHEN this pattern first appeared in the nineteenth century, it was known by a variety of names, usually depending on the region: Split Rail in Tennessee, Great Divide in Arkansas, and Rocky Mountain Road or Springtime in the Rockies in the West. In 1930, when the Stearns and Foster Company of Cincinnati included the pattern on its wrappers for Mountain Mist cotton batting, it was identified as New York Beauty, so that is how the quilt pattern is commonly known today.

This quilt was probably made by Rachel Muir, the mother of John Muir, who, along with his wife Ida, owned a sheep ranch near the mouth of the Marias River. John was born in Cleveland, Ohio, but Henry and Rachel Muir later moved their family to Indiana and then Texas. Rachel, by then probably a widow, again relocated her family around 1885. This time the Muirs settled for good in Montana. When Rachel died in Great Falls in 1920, John and Ida inherited Rachel's complicated and exquisite quilt; the Muirs, in turn, gave it to their daughter Cora Christine Shaw. The family called the quilt Railroad to the Rockies, adding yet another name to this pattern's lexicon.

Nineteenth-century New York Beauty quilts were often done in the color scheme of red and green on white, with occasional accents of orange and yellow. In this quilt the vibrant orange centers were created out of fabric colored with chrome orange, a mineral dye created by treating potassium dichromate with an alkali. The color became popular after it was produced commercially in the United States in the 1840s.

Railroad to the Rockies, Rachel Muir, mid-1800s,
MHQP 06-165-01 *(76" x 79", cotton)*

Lily

THIS beautiful Lily appliqué quilt has been a cherished family heirloom for more than a century and a half. Lydia Knox, wife of farmer Colton Knox, and their daughter Emeline stitched this quilt on the family farm in Kane County, Illinois. According to her great-granddaughter Edith McWilliams Murray, Lydia drew all the designs for the quilting, and Lydia and Emeline spent six months quilting it.

In 1862 Emeline married a local farmer and Methodist minister, William Whitfield Morrison, and the couple had seven children. Their oldest daughter Emily also married a farmer, William McWilliams, and in 1913 the McWilliamses decided to try their luck at homesteading in Montana. They packed their belongings, including this quilt, and traveled with their children and granddaughter to north-central Montana. "They took homesteads about eighteen miles west of Big Sandy," recounts Virginia Fox, Emily's granddaughter. "The wide open prairie of Montana was quite a change from the green Midwest they left."[8]

Although life was tough at first, the McWilliamses adapted to the open prairie. "When they first came their main source of meat was jack-rabbit or cottontail rabbit; then they gradually got chickens, pigs and cattle," writes Fox. "They raised wheat, barley, oats and corn and always had a big garden. The farming was done with horses until 1928 when they purchased a John Deere tractor. The first years were good and they could raise almost anything. Then the drought came!"[9]

This quilt has connected six generations of women since it was first made by Lydia Knox and her daughter Emeline. Initially, family tradition dictated that this quilt be passed from eldest daughter to eldest daughter: Emily McWilliams gave it to her daughter Edith McWilliams Murray; Edith bequeathed it to her daughter Helen Murray Bowman. But when Helen did not have any daughters, she gave the quilt to her sister Virginia Murray Fox of Fort Benton. Virginia also has no daughters, so she gave the quilt to her granddaughter Michelle Fox Salisbury of Missoula. Michelle is Lydia Knox's great-great-great-great-granddaughter.

LYDIA KNOX &
EMELINE KNOX
MORRISON

ca. 1852

Emily Morrison McWilliams inherited the Lily quilt made by her mother and grandmother. She is pictured on right with her sisters Jennie Morrison Caldwell (left) and Martha Morrison (center) on the Montana prairie, ca. 1913, when the McWilliams family homesteaded near Big Sandy.

*Lily, Lydia Knox and Emeline Knox Morrison,
ca. 1852, MHQP 19-20-01 (77" x 79", cotton)*

Flying Geese

JEMIMA THOMPSON

ca. 1860

JEMIMA Thompson, born in 1810, lived in New York State when she made this Flying Geese quilt, shortly before her death in 1863. Her great-great-granddaughter Catherine Kotesky of Great Falls, an avid quiltmaker herself, discovered this complex, richly hued quilt in a hope chest that she inherited upon her mother's death.

Although this pattern was published in the *Oklahoma Farmer Stockman* in 1929 under the name Flying Geese, early-twentieth-century quilt historians Nancy Cabot, Carrie Hall, and Rose Kretsinger all named this design Odd Fellows after the eighteenth-century English fraternal association that had spread to the United States by the 1850s.

It is unclear whether an association with the fraternity led Jemima to make this quilt or if she was instead inspired by nature's flying geese. She apparently ran out of time, materials, or patience and did not piece together enough squares to complete the edges. Although her decision to set the blocks "on point" (so they appear as diamonds rather than squares) followed a style that was popular in the first decades of the nineteenth century, she made the unusual decision to place the quarter and half squares kitty-cornered. This unique twist preserves the visual balance of the quilt when it is laid flat, although it would look asymmetrical draped across a bed.

In from the Fields, *by Robert F. Morgan (detail, 2007, oil on canvas), shows the flying V formation of geese that inspired the Flying Geese quilt pattern.*

Flying Geese, Jemima Thompson, ca. 1860, MHQP 02-57-01 *(64" x 81", cotton)*

THIS striking red-and-green Laurel Leaf quilt demonstrates two techniques that gained popularity after 1840: the use of appliqué and the preference for the color scheme of red and green, already a traditional color scheme in Pennsylvania Dutch folk art.

Quilt historian Nancy Hornback attributes the red-and-green craze in part to the advancements in dyeing technology. In the early nineteenth century, green fabric was produced from vegetable dyes. Fabric was dyed yellow over blue or blue over yellow, but over time one of the two colors usually faded. Around 1840 a colorfast green dye was developed, which made the fabric much more attractive to quiltmakers who wanted to create an appliqué masterpiece that could be passed down from generation to generation.

Vibrant red fabric was also more accessible by the late nineteenth century. The Turkey red process of dyeing (so-called because European dyers first discovered the technique in the eastern Mediterranean) had been simplified, which made it easier to commercially produce vibrant red fabric.

QUILTMAKER UNKNOWN

ca. 1860

A quilt with a similar Laurel Leaf motif is pictured on the left in this view of the music room of the Montana State Hospital in 1938.

Laurel Leaf, quiltmaker unknown, ca. 1860, MHQP 06-130-4 *(84" x 96", cotton)*

Pineapple, Alice Batchelder, ca. 1875, MHQP 19-25-01 (56" x 62", cotton, wool, silk)

Pineapple

ALICE BATCHELDER
ca. 1875

THIS intricate Pineapple quilt has been passed down by the women in Alice Batchelder's family, moving from cedar chest to cedar chest. The quilt was made by Alice Batchelder, the wife of physician Franklin P. Batchelder, of Clinton, Iowa. The Batchelders' eldest son Holmes moved to Montana sometime between 1900 and 1910. After first working on a sheep ranch in Ravalli County, Batchelder moved to Three Forks, where he and his wife Grace operated a creamery with their two sons Holmes Jr. and Bruce.

Grace Batchelder gave the quilt to her daughter-in-law Phoebe Black Batchelder, the wife of Holmes Jr., and for years it was stowed away in Phoebe's cedar chest. When Sue Lepley of Fort Benton inherited the quilt from Phoebe, her mother's sister, life was so hectic, she recalls, that she too "stored it in my cedar chest, never even unfolding it to see what I had. I honestly never saw the whole quilt until the ladies hung it up to measure it for [the Montana Historic Quilt Project] registration. Then I couldn't believe my eyes—it is beautiful!"[10] Someday Sue's daughter will inherit this heirloom.

Log Cabin quilts were popular among quilters in the second half of the nineteenth century, and the Pineapple block is a particularly complex variation of the Log Cabin technique. Other names for the Pineapple pattern include Windmill, Windmill Blades, and Maltese Cross.

Alice made an interesting choice in her use of red fabric for the center of her blocks. A long-cherished quilting myth holds that red placed at the center of Log Cabin blocks represented the hearth of the home. Some quiltmakers may have picked the color for its associations with warmth, but the abundance of historic Log Cabin quilts with different colored centers suggests that many quilters chose fabric colors on the basis of personal aesthetic and design rather than symbolism.

Alice gave the quilt to her daughter-in-law Grace, who, in turn, passed it to her daughter-in-law Phoebe, pictured here with her husband Holmes Batchelder Jr. in 1940. Phoebe passed the quilt on to their niece Sue Lepley, its current owner.

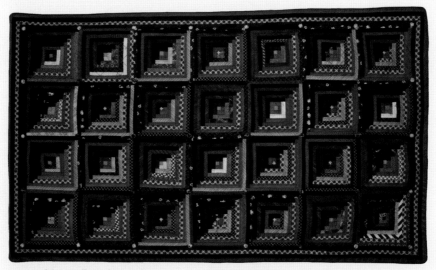

Log Cabin, quiltmaker unknown, ca. 1900, MHS X1981.01.14 (50" x 84", cotton, wool, silk). This is an example of the Log Cabin pattern from which the more complex Pineapple pattern is derived.

Delectable Mountains

GERTRUDE M. BAKER

1861

GERTRUDE M. Baker made this stunning Delectable Mountains quilt as her bridal quilt, in preparation for her 1861 marriage to John Baker. Popular in the 1840s and 1850s, Delectable Mountains quilts derived their name from the seventeenth-century allegory *The Pilgrim's Progress* by John Bunyan. Christian, the protagonist of Bunyan's work, escapes Doubting Castle, owned by the Giant Despair, and reaches the Delectable Mountains, owned by the Lord Emmanuel. These mountains are filled with "gardens and orchards, the vineyards and fountains of water," and from one of them Christian could see the gates of the Celestial City. The popularity of the Delectable Mountains pattern suggests the influence of Christianity on nineteenth-century quilting.

For Gertrude and John Baker, this Delectable Mountains quilt was a highly personal testament to their love. John drew the quilting designs, which feature the date of their marriage, Gertrude's initials, love knots, turtle doves, hearts, and flowers. The couple also embedded a quilted vision of their dream house in the fabric.

Gertrude and John passed the quilt down to their daughter, also named Gertrude M. Baker. A teacher in Fall River, Massachusetts, she lived for a time in an apartment at the home of her school's principal, Willard Henry Poole. Gertrude gave this quilt to Poole's daughter Phebe Poole Baxter, who brought it with her when she moved to Great Falls in 1977. An extraordinarily educated woman, Baxter graduated from Vassar in 1921 and received a master's degree in physics from Cornell in 1926. Throughout her life she also maintained an avid interest in genealogy, which explains why so much is known about this quilt's history.

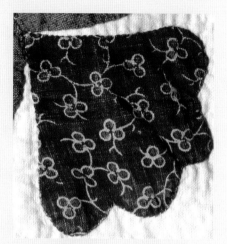

Delectable Mountains, Gertrude M. Baker, 1861, MHQP 02-46-01 (84" x 92", cotton)

Drunkard's Path, Eliza Ann Davis Robertson, 1861, MHQP 07-341-01 (66" x 76", cotton)

Drunkard's Path

ELIZA ANN DAVIS
ROBERTSON

1861

Eliza Ann Davis Robertson

ELIZA Ann Davis of Martinsburg, Iowa, hand-pieced the top for this Drunkard's Path quilt in 1861, just as the nation plunged into the Civil War. Her future husband John Robertson had enlisted in the Union army that same year, and before the war was over, he would be captured and taken to Andersonville, a Confederate prison camp notorious for its overcrowded, unsanitary conditions. Almost one-third of the men held there died, but John survived. For four generations, the family has preserved Eliza's quilt top, along with John's war medals and prison release papers. In 1999 Maridona Norick, the couple's great-granddaughter, commissioned the Risen Christ Quilters of Kalispell to complete the quilt.

The Drunkard's Path pattern has an interesting and controversial history. Authors Jacqueline Tobin and Raymond Dobard argue that quilts were used as signals for slaves escaping along the Underground Railroad. A Drunkard's Path quilt hanging on a clothesline, according to the authors, indicated that slaves needed to zigzag their escape route to evade capture. This thesis has come under heavy criticism from both quilt historians and scholars of African American history as being unsubstantiated and unrealistic, particularly because it relies heavily on the oral accounts with little corroborating historical evidence. Quilt historian Barbara Brackman articulates the difficulty of distinguishing between history and oral tradition: "We have no historical evidence of quilts being used as signals, codes, or maps. The tale of quilts and the Underground Railroad makes a good story, but not good quilt history."[11]

Even if the Drunkard's Path did not have a secret meaning during the Civil War, the design certainly took on political significance when it was adopted as a symbol of the Woman's Christian Temperance Union. The WCTU, founded in 1874, led one of the most powerful reform movements of the late nineteenth century. WCTU members made Drunkard's Path quilts in the organization's official colors of blue and white to demonstrate their allegiance to the movement and to raise money for its causes, which embraced not only temperance but suffrage, prison reform, and vocational training for women.

Lemoyne Star

AMANDA KELLEY HARTT

1864

THIS Lemoyne Star quilt traveled from Maine to Montana with Judah Hartt, son of Reverend John Hartt and Amanda Kelley Hartt. Amanda pieced the quilt top in 1864, but it was unfinished when she died in August 1869, just weeks after giving birth to her son Judah.

Judah, who married Canadian Jennie Dunham around 1893, took the quilt top with him when he moved his young family west, first to Sheridan, Montana, and then to Butte, where he worked in the mines. Judah's wife Jennie and other women in the family completed the quilt around the turn of the century, most likely while they were still living in Montana. The Hartts returned to Maine for a time and then came back to the West around 1910, this time to try their hand at sheep ranching in Wyoming.

While Judah and Jennie lived out the rest of their days in Wyoming, Amanda's quilt made its way back to Montana. Jennie and Judah's second son John bequeathed the quilt to his daughter Shirley Lindell, who was living in Fort Benton when she registered the quilt with the Montana Historic Quilt Project in 1995.

Ruth Finley, in her 1929 book *Old Patchwork Quilts and the Women Who Made Them*, suggested that the Lemoyne Star pattern took its name from brothers Pierre Le Moyne d'Iberville and Jean-Baptist Le Moyne de Bienville, French explorers who sailed into the Gulf of Mexico and rediscovered the mouth of the Mississippi. The brothers led the first effort to colonize Louisiana in 1699, and Jean-Baptist helped found the city of New Orleans in 1718. They also are often credited with bringing the celebration of Mardi Gras to Louisiana, although it is not clear why this popular quilt is named in their honor. Outside Louisiana, the name occasionally has been shortened to Lemon Star.

Amanda's Lemoyne Star incorporates some lovely old fabrics, including an unusual double-pink background. Double pinks, as Eileen Jahnke Trestain explains, were produced from 1850 to the early 1900s and were "made by printing several layers of pink, rose, or red over one another to create the appearance at a distance of a solid color, but on close examination a textured pink can be seen."[12]

Amanda's son Judah Hartt brought this Lemoyne Star quilt top to Montana; his wife Jennie and other women in the family completed the quilt ca. 1900.

Lemoyne Star, Amanda Kelley Hartt, 1864, MHQP 19-03-01 (78" x 92", cotton)

Red and Green Sampler, quiltmaker unknown, ca. 1870, MHQP 02-44-01 *(80" x 81", cotton)*

Red and Green Sampler

QUILTMAKER UNKNOWN

ca. 1870

THIS sampler is a fine example of the red-and-green quilts that were so popular in the second half of the nineteenth century, in part because they offered quiltmakers the opportunity to showcase their appliqué and quilting skills. According to the *Encyclopedia of Applique*, Barbara Brackman's indispensable guide to identifying and dating quilts, several of the quilt's wreath blocks resemble those on an 1870s quilt in the collection of the Shelburne Museum in Vermont. The designs on other blocks appear to be original. Along with the elaborate outline quilting, the quiltmaker added dimension to this quilt by stuffing some of the berries and flowers.

A family friend gave this sampler to Maria Winslow of Great Falls, and all Maria knows about the quilt is that it was made in Muncy, Pennsylvania, by "a cousin of Dr. Farr in Billings." Based on census records, the Dr. Farr in question very likely was Dr. Eri Farr, who was born in Muncy in 1884 but moved in 1913 to Billings, the town where his new wife Laura Fish had been raised. Doctor Farr was, according to *Montana, Its Story and Biography*, "One of the skilled and reliable physicians and surgeons of Billings . . . whose reputation is not merely a local one, but extends over a wide territory, and he is oftentimes called into consultation by his brother practitioners." The piece glowingly concluded: "Possessing as he does the characteristics which make for good citizenship, he has always been considered as one of the best types of American manhood . . . and the influence he wields is not inconsiderable."[13]

Red and Green, Mrs. Henry Riley Johnson, 1830–1850, MHS 1999.18.01, MHQP 02-77-01 (73" x 84", cotton). This is another example of the popular color scheme.

Sunburst

MARGURITE MURPHY

ca. 1870

MARGURITE Murphy made this incredible Sunburst quilt around 1870, and the prizewinning heirloom has been passed down through the family ever since. Born in Tennessee around 1817, Margurite married farmer Robert Murphy. Just before the start of the Civil War, the couple moved their family from Tennessee to Somerset, Kentucky.

Their eldest son Moses Murphy fought under Confederate general John Hunt Morgan before being captured and held as a prisoner of war for twenty-one months. At the war's close, Moses returned to Kentucky. He married Sarah Elizabeth Richardson in 1867, and in 1898 Sarah, Moses, and their two sons took the Northern Pacific Railroad across the plains to Montana to try their luck at homesteading in Broadwater County. They stayed on the farm for twenty-six years, until Moses retired, and then the couple moved into Townsend, where he died in 1923 and she, the next year.

According to the family, Moses entered his mother's Sunburst quilt in the Gallatin County Fair in the early 1900s, and it won first prize. Moses gave the quilt to his daughter Carey Bowler, who in turn passed it along to her niece and Moses's granddaughter Grace Melton. Grace registered the quilt with the Montana Historic Quilt Project before she passed away in 1999. Her nephew William Gillespie of Toston, recognizing the quilt's extraordinary craftsmanship and its place in Montana's pioneer history, donated it to the Museum of the Rockies in Bozeman in 2007.

Sunburst, Margurite Murphy, ca. 1870, MHQP 06-64-01 (82" x 83", cotton)

Nine Patch, Mary Elizabeth Brown Ransdell Lord and Friends, ca. 1875,
MHS 1999.56.184 (69" x 96", cotton)

Nine Patch

MARY ELIZABETH
BROWN RANSDELL LORD
& FRIENDS

ca. 1875

THIS Nine-Patch quilt was made for Mary "Minnie" Shelton Ransdell Churchill, possibly as a gift to celebrate her marriage to D. H. Churchill in 1875. When a Churchill family descendant donated the quilt to the Montana Historical Society in 1999, it was attributed to Mathilda Price Churchill, D. H. Churchill's stepmother. The quilt, however, had another story to tell. Curators at the Montana Historical Society found clues indicating that it was instead pieced by Minnie's mother Mary Elizabeth Brown Ransdell Lord. After the quilt was constructed, Mary Lord's mother, sister, and children from her second marriage—Minnie's stepbrothers and stepsisters—helped to hand-quilt the gift. They also wrote personal notes to Minnie and pinned them to the quilt.

Because it was quilted by a group rather than an individual, this Nine Patch represents a beloved tradition: the quilting party, or "bee." Quilting bees did occur in the nineteenth century, but their frequency has been greatly exaggerated, perhaps because they encapsulate cherished notions of the past. Quilting bees evoke scenes of neighbors helping neighbors, and women getting together to exchange recipes, talk about their children, and gossip about the menfolk. In truth, most women probably quilted alone, especially if they were working on intricate pieces and wanted to control the quality of the quilting.

One of Minnie Churchill's stepbrothers wrote "Dick the Bum, I done the Best I Could" on a note pinned to the quilt, likely her wedding gift, that he had helped stitch.

Although quilting parties may not have occurred as often as we would like to think, the quilting on this Nine Patch was done collectively so the whole family could contribute to Mary's wedding gift to Minnie. One unusual aspect of this quilting party was that men participated. One of Minnie's step-brothers wrote, "Dear Sister You will observe on the NorthEast corner some Batchelor Stitches which was made by the hand of Chas. E. Lord." Charles seemed to be rather proud of his contribution, but another of the men who aided in the quilting felt the need to apologize for his work. He wrote, "Dick the Bum, I done the Best I Could."

Eagles, Maria Nestlerode or Martha Elizabeth Nestlerode Smith, ca. 1876, MHQP 02-26-03 *(72" x 73", cotton)*

Eagles

MARIA NESTLERODE
OR MARTHA ELIZABETH
NESTLERODE SMITH

ca. 1876

THIS striking eagle appliqué quilt was made by Maria Nestlerode or her daughter Martha Elizabeth Nestlerode Smith in Beech Creek, Pennsylvania. When Beth Duke of Great Falls cleaned out her grandfather's house in Beech Creek, she found this and several other quilts. Beth and her sisters Shelley Smith, Susan Zelensky, and Lynn Smith have extensively researched their family history and believe that several of the women in their family quilted. According to family tradition, the women pieced the quilts alone in the summer and then gathered together in the fall to quilt while the men went hunting.

This eagle appliqué pattern does not have a name, but quilt historian Barbara Brackman has found that it was particularly popular in Pennsylvania around 1880. That eagles appeared frequently on quilts at that time is no surprise. The United States had just celebrated its centennial, which sparked a flurry of quilts featuring patriotic themes. In addition to solid-colored appliqués such as this one, quilters displayed their love of country by using a broad array of Americana-inspired fabrics that featured national symbols like the American flag and the Liberty Bell. Ethnicity, as well as patriotism, may also have influenced the choice of the eagle appliqué. "The popularity of the eagle in Pennsylvania may be due to its strong German heritage," notes Brackman. "In some German religious traditions, the eagle with its spread wings represented God's protection."[14]

The centennial of the Lewis and Clark Expedition sparked a wave of patriotism in 1904–1906. The New Home Sewing Machine Company celebrated the event with this 1904 advertisement featuring a map of the Louisiana Purchase, portraits of Napoleon and Thomas Jefferson, and Old Glory.

Crazy

MARY Ann Wight Parks made this one-of-a-kind Crazy quilt in Iowa, and she brought it along when she and her husband Tom moved to Montana Territory in 1882. The Parkses followed the lead of Mary's brother Alex, who had already established a homestead at Stone Station near Philipsburg. At the time they moved, Mary was pregnant with the couple's eldest daughter Lala Francis. Lala later inherited this quilt and two others made by her mother, and the family has continued the tradition of passing Mary's quilts down to the eldest daughter.

As this elaborate quilt suggests, Mary was a passionate artist. She used the fabric as a canvas for both painting and embroidery. Although this quilt was intended only for display, Mary also made more utilitarian quilts, such as the Churn Dash pictured below.

Mary Ann Wight Parks and her daughter Lala Francis Blanche Parks (Carey), ca. 1889

(above) *Churn Dash, Mary Ann Wight Parks, ca. 1889,* MHQP 04-90-01 (80" x 80", cotton)

(opposite) *Crazy, Mary Ann Wight Parks, ca. 1870,* MHQP 04-90-02 (64" x 80", silk, wool, linen)

AMERICA Victoria Wilhite Kent made this Seven Sisters hexagon quilt around the same time she and her husband William moved from Missouri to Montana Territory. According to the family, the Kents took the steamboat *Far West* up the Missouri River to Fort Benton in the late 1870s. They then traveled by wagon from Fort Benton to Bozeman, where they settled down to farm and raise cattle.

Shortly after the birth of their youngest child, William was fatally scalded in a steam-engine accident, leaving America to raise their twelve children and manage the ranch. With her oldest son's help, America succeeded for a time; she even managed to purchase a home in Bozeman so that her children could attend college. But in 1910 she sold her property in Gallatin County and moved east to Hardin, where eventually she "lost everything she had" as drought swept over the plains.[15]

AMERICA VICTORIA
WILHITE KENT

ca. 1880

Seven Sisters, America Victoria Wilhite Kent, ca. 1880, MHQP 22-05-02 (72" x 93", cotton)

The Kent family came to Montana on the steamboat Far West, *pictured here in 1880 at Cow Island, a stop on the Missouri River below Fort Benton.*

Crazy, Pamelia Fergus, Luella Fergus Gilpatrick, and Mary Agnes Fergus Hamilton, ca. 1880, MHQP 06-115-1 (33" x 41", silk, velvet)

Crazy

PAMELIA FERGUS,
LUELLA FERGUS
GILPATRICK &
MARY AGNES FERGUS
HAMILTON

ca. 1880

SHORTLY before her hundredth birthday, Hazel Akeley Fergus gave this lovely but unfinished Crazy quilt top to her granddaughter Charlotte Quigley Orr of Lewistown. The top had been given to Hazel by her new sisters-in-law Luella Fergus Gilpatrick and Mary Agnes Fergus Hamilton when she married Andrew Fergus in 1909.

Luella and Agnes began piecing this Crazy quilt around 1880 with their mother Pamelia Fergus, who died from breast cancer seven years later. The quilt was never completed, but the top has been cherished by her family because it is a material reminder of the life of one of Montana's most extraordinary pioneer women, a life that has been the subject of both an original opera—Eric Funk's *Pamelia*—and the inspiration for a book—Linda Peavy and Ursula Smith's *The Gold Rush Widows of Little Falls*.

Born in 1824 in upstate New York, Pamelia Dillin married Scotsman James Fergus in Moline, Illinois, in 1845. Because James's business endeavors often took him away from home, Pamelia raised their four children, ran their household, and often managed her husband's business holdings on her own. In 1860 James left his family in Little Falls, Minnesota, to seek his fortune in the goldfields of Colorado. His quest for gold had taken him north to Montana by 1862, and a year later he finally struck it rich in the diggings at Alder Gulch.

James's good fortune was a mixed blessing for Pamelia, who had to leave her friends in Little Falls and relocate her family. As she made plans and purchased supplies for the journey, the one thing Pamelia wanted most was a sewing machine. After agonizing over which model to choose, she ordered a Wheeler and Wilson in January 1864.

In his letters to Pamelia, James had given his blessing to the purchase of a sewing machine, but he discouraged her from bringing other bulky items, such as furniture, dishes, and old clothing. Peavy and Smith recount his advice on the matter of bedding: "Oblivious to the value a quilt had for the woman who had made it or had received it from her mother's or grandmother's hands, he wrote, 'Quilts don't answer very well on the road. They get torn too easy.' This was no time to think of favorite items whose sentimental value did not justify transporting them across the plains."[16]

In August 1864 Pamelia met James in Virginia City, but the couple bounced around Lewis and Clark County in the following years, moving from Last Chance Gulch to a Prickly Pear Valley ranch to their son Andrew's ranch and stage station near Silver City. In 1880 Pamelia had finally settled down in Helena, where she and her daughters probably began piecing this quilt top. Later that year, however, Pamelia moved one final time to a large ranch near present-day Lewistown, north of the Judith Mountains, where James had relocated his cattle holdings.

Pamelia Fergus (above, ca. 1884) made the Crazy quilt with her daughters Frances Luella Fergus Gilpatrick (below, left) and Mary Agnes Fergus Hamilton (below, right). Her son Andrew is also pictured.

CHAPTER TWO

Statehood & Settlement | 1889 TO 1919

Montana officially became the forty-first state in the Union on November 8, 1889, and it was copper mining that drove the economy of the new state. By the 1890s, Montana produced over 40 percent of the nation's copper, and many of the state's political controversies of the period—including the placement of the state capital and Montana's choice for U.S. senator—centered on the inimical relationship between Copper Kings Marcus Daly and William A. Clark. The mining boom, coupled with the arrival of three transcontinental railroads, the Northern Pacific and Great Northern, and later the Milwaukee Road, drew diverse new groups to the state. The state's population soared as Irish and Cornishmen, Finns, Chinese, Italians, and eastern European Slavs came to work in the Butte mines or the smelters and refineries at Anaconda, Black Eagle, and East Helena. Communities such as Billings, Livingston, Malta, and Kalispell grew up ovenight as entrepreneurs platted new towns along the rail lines.

Flying Geese, Ella Hardin, ca. 1898, MHS *1990.41.01 (pieced, 80" x 95", cotton).*
Ella Hardin arrived in Miles City in the 1890s on a cattle drive from Texas.

Quilting party, Choteau, March 10, 1901, including (back row from left): Grace Vance Erickson, Mrs. Gorham, Mrs. Charles L. Cooper, Mrs. O. G. Cooper, unidentified; (front row from left): Mrs. Clair Drake, Mrs. Garvin, Mrs. Cunningham

While mining dominated the state politically in the early years of statehood, agriculture transformed Montana's rural landscape. By the turn of the century, the open ranges of eastern Montana had been fenced, and prosperous small farms dotted the fertile valleys of the Bitterroot, Jefferson, Gallatin, and other western Montana rivers. Still, vast tracts of public land in the eastern two-thirds of the state remained unsettled. Up until 1901, homesteaders came into Montana in a trickle: each year fewer than one thousand people filed for patents on homestead land. The homesteading boom changed that. In the second decade of the twentieth century, settlers filed more than one hundred thousand new claims on Montana lands.

Two things—the doctrine of dryland farming and the Enlarged Homestead Act of 1909, which increased the size of homestead claims from 160 to 320 acres—encouraged aspiring farmers to migrate to Montana's eastern plains. In the eastern part of the state, most areas received fewer than fourteen inches of rain, too little to grow crops without irrigation. Dryland farming proponents, however, argued that if farmers used such techniques as soil compaction and summer fallowing, "rain would follow the plow." The most famous advocate of dryfarming, Hardy Webster Campbell, wrote in 1909 that the prairies of eastern Montana and the Dakotas were "destined to be the last and best grain gardenry of the world."[1]

Real estate speculators, newspaper editors, chambers of commerce, government officials, and, above all, railroad interests championed dryland farming. In the early part of the decade, this optimism seemed justified. Montana experienced unusually ample rainfall in the 1910s, averaging sixteen inches of precipitation per year between 1909 and 1916. Times were good: the federal government set the price of wheat at around $2.20 per bushel during World War I, and in the wettest years of 1915–1916 many northern Montana farms produced thirty-five to fifty bushels per acre. In response to this economic bonanza, banks offered easy access to credit, which allowed farmers to buy more land and equipment.

Even during these good years, however, farming required constant toil. When recalling her parents' experiences on their High Line homestead, Mary Kindzerski summarized it succinctly: "All their life, they just kept working."[2] Many homesteaders lived in crude sod houses or small lumber shacks, and they might travel miles to gather wood or water. Of course, the task of running the household largely fell to women. They cooked on wood or coal stoves, laundered in hard water, and tended the garden while minding children and mending clothes. For many homesteader women, stitching lush Crazy quilts, intricate patchwork quilts, or bold Log Cabin quilts was a way, perhaps, of bringing beauty into their difficult lives.

(left) "Mabel Williams brings water to the threshing crew at work on her family's farm in September, 1909."

(below) Rosie Roesler's homestead, August 31, 1913

Given the demands on their time, it is remarkable the extent to which many homesteaders stayed connected to local and national events through periodicals. For instance, in a March 1914 letter to her mother in Indiana, Maggie Gorman Davis, who homesteaded with her husband near Carter, wrote that their household received *McCall's, Homelife, American Woman, Housewife,* and *Women's World* as well as *Successful Farming, Dakota Farmer,* and three weekly newspapers.[3] In the early 1910s, one of the newspaper stories Montanans followed most closely was the effort to bring voting rights to Montana women, an endeavor led by a young woman from a prominent Missoula family, Jeannette Rankin.

Rankin—who, interestingly enough, was a talented seamstress and who after graduating from the University of Montana in 1902 had earned a living taking in sewing—learned about progressive issues as a social worker in New York and cut her political teeth working for women's suffrage in Washington State. In 1911 she brought her political skills back to her home state. That year the Montana legislature considered but rejected a bill that would give women the vote. Following the defeat, Rankin and her fellow suffragists organized the Montana Equal Suffrage Association, and in 1913 women's suffrage had enough support in the legislature to garner the two-thirds majority vote required to amend the state constitution. Only a referendum was required for the amendment to become law. Rankin campaigned relentlessly, traveling a total of six thousand miles to drum up support for the amendment. On November 3, 1914, Montanans granted women the right to vote by a narrow margin of 41,302 to 37,588. The clout of the new female voters was already apparent in the elections held two years later: two women won seats in the state legislature, one was selected as superintendent of public instruction, and Jeannette Rankin became the first woman elected to the U.S. Congress.

Montanans broke new ground in sending Jeannette Rankin to Congress. In the world of quilting, however, Montana was on par with the rest of the country, as quilting tastes were becoming increasingly homogenized nationwide. This standardization of quilting can be traced over the course of the nineteenth century. In the early 1800s pattern-sharing among neighbors and family members was the norm, and these exchanges resulted in the development of regional quilting traditions. As print media became more widespread, however, this regional diversity diminished. More and more women drew their quilting inspiration from national ladies' magazines. Even rural women without easy access to stores could duplicate the quilts they saw in magazines with fabrics ordered from mail-order catalogs such as Montgomery Ward's (which began offering "Cotton Prints" in its very first catalog published in 1872); Bloomingdale Brothers; and Sears, Roebuck and Company.

Even more significant than the rise of the mail-order catalog was the sewing machine, which transformed women's domestic work. First patented in 1846, the sewing machine was the first appliance available on an installment plan, which put it within reach of women who might not otherwise be able to buy one. Women who had previously spent the bulk of their days sewing looked upon the machine as a "miraculous timesaver," and it is not surprising that the use of sewing machines spread rapidly. By the early 1900s, according to quilt historians Thomas Woodward and Blanche Greenstein, the sewing machine "had found its way into even most rural homes."[4]

Montana women were not removed from the influence of the sewing machine. Some immigrants, such as

Sewing machine ad, Montgomery Ward & Co.'s catalog, 1895

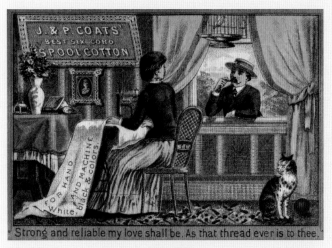

Thread advertisement, ca. 1885–1895

By the 1910s quilting began regaining popularity nationally. About the same time, illustrator Coles Phillips introduced his "fadeaway girl" technique that appeared on magazine covers, poster, and in ads. Here he combined her with a Basket quilt, ca. 1912.

Pamelia Fergus, whose Crazy quilt was pictured in the previous chapter, considered a sewing machine so vital to life on the frontier that they brought their machines with them. Other women bought sewing machines after arriving in their new home. In an advertisement in the May 15, 1874, *Helena Daily Independent*, Robert J. Mulligan & Co. offered a range of sewing machines costing between ten and eighty dollars with "NO EXTRA CHARGES made for packing or shipping to ANY PART OF THE COUNTRY." The ad, incidentally, bragged that its eighty-dollar machine "Will do every description of sewing, HEM, FELL, TUCK SEAM, QUILT."[5] Demand must

have been high because just one month later, in June 1874, the Helena paper noted that "J. W. Corey, traveling agent of the Singer Sewing Machine Company, is in town in the interest of his company." At the end of the month, the Singer Manufacturing Company took out another newspaper advertisement to announce it had opened an office at the J. R. Boyce and Company dry-goods store and was sending out agents to "visit all the towns and principal valleys in the Territory this summer and fall." By 1876 Singer had also established an office and showroom in Butte.[6]

It is difficult to judge just how many Montana women had sewing machines in the 1880s and 1890s. That a fair number of early Helenans owned one is demonstrated by A. B. Charpel's 1876 *Helena Daily Independent* advertisement announcing, "The repairing of Sewing Machines made a specialty." Another piece in the *Daily Independent*, "Essay on Women," hinted that machine-sewn garments marked a rural-urban divide. In the article the author warned men against "bad women" like that ultimate "bad girl" Eve: "Eve was like the rest of

Christian Cross, quiltmaker unknown, ca. 1895, MHQP 03-16-03, WHC 95.02.01 *(detail, pieced, 71" x 72", cotton)*

her sisters: just tell her not to do a thing, and she would be sure to do it. Eve must have been a country girl. She didn't care much for fashion, and she made her own clothes, without a sewing machine. She would be rather behind the times should she visit us now."[7]

By the turn of the century, it is clear that the sewing machine had changed the way women made clothing and household goods. That it had also changed the way some women quilted can be seen from the machine-pieced wool Crazy quilt pictured on page 99

that was made around the turn of the century by May Baxter Vestal, who lived in the small rural community of Two Dot. Despite the availability of sewing machines, however, many Montana quiltmakers continued to piece and quilt by hand. Although machines certainly made sewing chores easier and faster, quilting was not a necessity or a chore; it was an art and a luxury, and many women simply preferred making quilts by hand.

Quiltmaking continued to enjoy popularity in Montana during the first decade of the new century even as nationally quilting became less fashionable, especially for women living in cities. World War I, however, reversed this trend as ladies' magazines encouraged women to take up quilting as a way to help on the home front by saving blankets "for our boys over there."[8] The American Red Cross also promoted quilting as a way for women to contribute to the war effort. Women around the country made Red Cross quilts, raising money by selling spaces on the quilt for signatures. Interestingly, this quiltmaking fervor did not end with the Great War. The women who quilted to help "make the world safe for democracy" were at the fore of a quiltmaking revival that would last through the Great Depression. But that is a story for another chapter. ❖

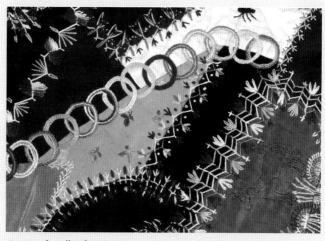

Scrap quilt (detail, pieced), Hattie and Bessie Preble, ca. 1910, MHQP 22-180-02. *See full quilt on page xv.*

Crazy, detail, Ida May Brust, ca. 1900, MHQP 07-214-01. *See full quilt on page vi.*

MINNIE Fligelman used velvet and silk samples from her husband Herman's merchandise cart to make this Crazy quilt, according to her daughters Frieda Fligelman and Belle Fligelman Winestine, who donated this quilt to the Montana Historical Society in 1949. Minnie died while giving birth to Belle in 1891, when Frieda was only one year old. This quilt was a beautiful and cherished memento of the mother Frieda and Belle never knew.

Minnie Weinzweig and Herman Fligelman, both Romanian Jews, married in Minnesota in 1888 or 1889. In 1889 they moved to Helena, where Herman ran the New York Dry Goods Company. He was a prominent figure in early Helena. A tribute that appeared in the *Helena Daily Independent* shortly after his death in June 1932 lauded him as "a real merchant who would serve people alike in good times and bad. He would sell them honest goods for honest prices and take their money when they had it, or sell them what they needed and see them through hard winters when they were without means."[9]

Perhaps even more extraordinary were the lives of Herman's two extremely accomplished daughters. Frieda Fligelman received her bachelor's degree from the University of Wisconsin. She successfully completed her written and oral doctoral exams at Columbia before having her dissertation rejected because of her controversial field of study, linguistic sociology. Without a doctorate, Frieda could not secure a position at a large research university, so she spent her life as an independent scholar in her hometown. After finding that "putting 'Helena, Montana' on her name tag at scientific conventions was repelling people who thought that great minds belonged in greater cities, she began to designate herself the 'Institute of Social Logic.'" With Frieda as both its "director and staff," the "Institute" ran out of Frieda's second-story apartment until her death in 1978.[10]

Younger sister Belle also attended the University of Wisconsin, where she served as president of the Women's Student Government Association and editor of the women's page of the student newspaper. When she returned to Montana, Belle became one of the state's first female reporters and an ardent activist for suffrage. She later recalled her stepmother Getty's reaction to her political outspokenness: "While it was all right for women to vote, she said, no respectable lady would speak on a street corner. She warned me that if I made one more speech on the street, I needn't come home. That night I slept in a hotel and charged it to my father."[11] During the suffrage campaign, Belle and Jeannette Rankin became acquainted, and in 1916 Belle accompanied the newly elected congresswoman to Washington as her legislative aide. In 1932 Belle, who was by then married to Norman Winestine, ran for the state senate. Although unsuccessful in her bid for office, Belle continued to write and champion women's rights throughout her life. In 1999 the *Missoulian* honored Belle as one of the one hundred most influential Montanans of the twentieth century.

Minnie Fligelman, 1889

Fligelman's New York Dry Goods Store, Helena, ca. 1890

*(opposite) Crazy, Minnie Fligelman, 1889, MHS X1949.04.01
(20" x 34", satin, damask, velvet)*

CLARA "Carrie" Mulholland Slater made this brightly colored Nine-Patch variation sometime around the turn of the century. Born in Ontario in 1848, Clara married Peter Slater in 1867, and the couple later moved from Ontario to farm in Campbell, Michigan. They had eight children, three of whom died in infancy. Clara was not only a devoted mother and caring wife, noted an article celebrating the Slaters' sixtieth wedding anniversary, she was also a hard worker who "spent many a day on the end of a crosscut saw."[12] In 1906 the Slaters sold their farm and retired to Freeport, Michigan.

Clara's daughter Minnie Slater Burleigh moved to Great Falls with her husband Frank in 1896. Sometime in the 1930s a family member sent several of her mother's quilts and other family treasures to Minnie in a trunk, and later, Minnie's granddaughter Frances Wylder inherited the quilts made by her great-grandmother. After carefully preserving them for almost forty years, Fran donated the quilts to the History Museum in Great Falls.

The Letter X quilt pattern Clara used for the quilt was published by the Ladies Art Company in 1897. Founded in 1889 by H. M. Brocksted, the Ladies Art Company initially sold scraps of silk, velvet, and plush for Crazy quilts, but by 1895 it also sold quilt patterns in its catalog. It is often credited as the first mail-order quilt pattern company, although research by quilt historian Wilene Smith has indicated that the Modern Art Company of New Haven, Connecticut, might have started publishing patterns earlier. The Ladies Art Company remained in business for almost a century, publishing hundreds of patterns and coining many of the names still associated with quilt blocks today.

Clara "Carrie" Mulholland Slater is seated second from right, next to her husband Peter, on their sixtieth anniversary in 1927. The others are their sons and daughters, including Minnie Slater Burleigh, standing, the quilt owner's grandmother, who moved to Montana in 1896.

*Letter X Variation, Clara "Carrie" Mulholland Slater, 1880–1900,
MHQP 02-30-01 (64" x 78", cotton)*

Crazy

MARY A. KIRBY
1893

OCCASIONALLY quilts capture moments in history more vividly than diaries or letters. This Crazy quilt, made by Mary A. Kirby of Livingston in 1893, documents the battle to choose the permanent location of the Montana state capital, incorporating silk ribbons bearing the names of the competing towns.

The 1889 Montana Constitution left the permanent location of the state capital to a popular vote. Because investors could make fortunes if their town was chosen, the fight for the Montana capital was extremely contentious. The first election was held in 1892 (a runoff election, in 1894, would ultimately decide the question). At the time, political candidates commonly printed campaign ribbons because they were relatively inexpensive and easily pinned to supporters' lapels. After the election the ribbons became novel keepsakes. In the 1892 election, town promoters were profligate with these pieces of silk: Mary's quilt incorporates ribbons from Anaconda, Boulder, Bozeman, Butte, Deer Lodge, Great Falls, and Helena.

Mary Kirby was born in Canada in 1849 and immigrated to the United States in 1865. She married William Kirby around 1882, and the couple farmed for a time in Iowa but had moved to Montana by 1900. Mary died in 1907. In 1962 her historically significant quilt was donated to the Montana Historical Society by her granddaughter Oscia MacGinniss of Salt Lake City, Utah.

Crazy, Mary A. Kirby, 1893, MHS X1962.11.01 *(71" x 90", cotton, silk, satin, corduroy)*

Four Patch

OLGA GREEN

1890–1920

ON the surface, Olga Green's Four-Patch quilt, meticulously hand-pieced from tiny scraps of fabric, seems to represent the ideal of frugality, one of the most cherished myths about quilting, especially since the Great Depression. Certainly some quiltmakers were careful to use every scrap of fabric they could. In the thirty-first edition of her popular advice book, *The American Frugal Housewife*, Lydia Maria Child explained the thriftiness of patchwork: "The true economy of housekeeping is simply the art of gathering up all the fragments, so that nothing is lost. I mean fragments of *time*, as well as *materials*. Nothing should be thrown away so long as it is possible to make any use of it, however trifling that use may be. . . . In this point of view, patchwork is good economy. It is indeed a foolish waste of time to tear cloth into bits for the sake of arranging it anew in fantastic figures; but a large family may be kept out of idleness, and a few shillings saved, by thus using scraps of gowns, curtains, &c."[13]

Yet for all their association with thrift, quilts pieced from leftover scraps were more the exception than the rule. Quilts were not cheap to make, no matter the materials used. They required significant expenditures for fabric and thread, particularly when appliqué became popular in the second half of the nineteenth century. Even after American fabrics became less expensive and more accessible at the end of the nineteenth century, the financial resources required to purchase quilting materials meant that many quilts were out of reach of the "frugal housewife."

Olga's Four Patch—though it did not "waste" fabric through overlap in the way that appliqué did—still required significant amounts of cloth for the seam allowances. It also was not constructed entirely from scraps, as Olga would have needed quite a bit of the red fabric she used for the alternating blocks.

(*opposite*) Four Patch, Olga Green, 1890–1920, MHQP 04-12-09 (68" x 73", cotton). (*above*) Nine Patch, Mary Wells Gump, 1890–1900, MHS 1992.24.04 (66" x 80", cotton, wool). *Both quilters used scraps and leftovers as well as new fabric.*

Crazy, Laura Van Leeuwen Kruse, 1893, MHQP 06-62-01 *(68" x 78", silk, satin, velvet)*

Crazy

LAURA VAN LEEUWEN
KRUSE

1893

THE Montana Historic Quilt Project researchers were stunned by the discovery of this gorgeous, carefully planned, and beautifully executed sixteen-point medallion quilt and the two nineteen-inch square pillow shams accompanying it. The quilt was made by Laura Van Leeuwen Kruse, who was born in Holland but spent most of her life in Minnesota and California. Jan Schwartz, Laura's great niece, inherited the quilt from her mother and registered it with the Montana Historic Quilt Project while living in Bozeman.

According to the family, this quilt won first prize at the 1893 World's Columbian Exposition in Chicago. The Columbian Exposition was a world's fair that commemorated the four-hundredth anniversary of Christopher Columbus's landfall in America, and it included a Women's Building to display the arts and handcrafts of the fairer sex.

Struck by the number of people who claimed their historic quilts won "first prize" at the fair, quilt historian Barbara Brackman searched for an authoritative list of prizewinners at the Columbian Exposition. When she consulted the exhibits list, Brackman found "1 bedspread" and "5 slumber quilts," all, interestingly enough, from Montana. However, she did not find a list of the prize-winning quilts. She concluded: "The image of a World's Fair as a County Fair on a grand scale is wrong. [It] . . . was not a contest, but an exhibit. Diplomas of Honorable Mention were awarded in the Women's Building to selected exhibits. These were conferred by the Board of Lady Managers upon 'designers, inventors and expert artisans . . . in recognition of the highest class of work.' Apparently several were given out in each category. . . . However, in Category 104 (Lace, Embroideries, Trimmings, Artificial Flowers, Fans, etc.) there were no quilts listed as holders of diplomas."[14] Brackman's findings suggest that Laura Kruse's spectacular quilt probably did not take home first prize, although it is quite possible that it was displayed there.

Laura Kruse, ca. 1880s

Pillow sham

Log Cabin

MARGUERITE "MARGARET"
McCLEERY ALVORD

1893

THIS lovely Log Cabin quilt was made by Marguerite "Margaret" McCleery Alvord, wife of Lieutenant Benjamin Alvord, while he was stationed at Fort Assinniboine, near present-day Havre, which had been built in 1879 to protect against attack by the Lakota Sioux who had slipped across the Canadian border after the Battle of the Little Bighorn. Margaret made at least three Crazy quilts and two other silk Log Cabin quilts around 1893, possibly piecing them with other officers' wives. All of the quilts were donated to the Montana Historical Society in 2005 by the Alvords' great-grandson Reginald Rutherford III and his wife Karen Jensen Rutherford. It is telling that Margaret chose to stitch these show quilts rather than something more utilitarian; they may have been a way to bring a semblance of Victorian gentility to her life on the northern plains. Since few records from the fort exist today, Margaret's quilts are not only beautiful mementoes but also important historical artifacts.

One of the married officers' quarters at Fort Assinniboine

Log Cabin quilts were extremely popular from the 1870s through the 1890s. The squares were traditionally made by sewing strips around a center square, alternating between light and dark fabrics. The squares were then sewn together in a variety of combinations to produce different visual effects, and Margaret's version is sometimes called Light and Dark. Once thought to be the quintessential American quilt because it evoked the warmth of the hearth and pioneer values, the Log Cabin design actually may have originated in the British Isles, possibly inspired by a similar motif appearing in Roman tiles and Egyptian mummy wrappings.

Like Crazy quilts of the same era, Log Cabin quilts made from velvets and silks were meant to be displayed rather than used as bedding. Silk show quilts became particularly popular in the United States in the late nineteenth century, and American textile manufacturers quickly capitalized on the popularity of this Asian fabric. By 1900 mills were using silk thread imported from China to weave two-thirds of the world's silk cloth.

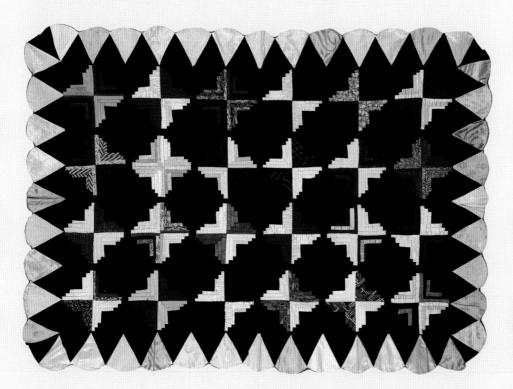

Log Cabin, Marguerite "Margaret" McCleery Alvord, 1893, MHS 2006.14.03 (38" x 53", silk)

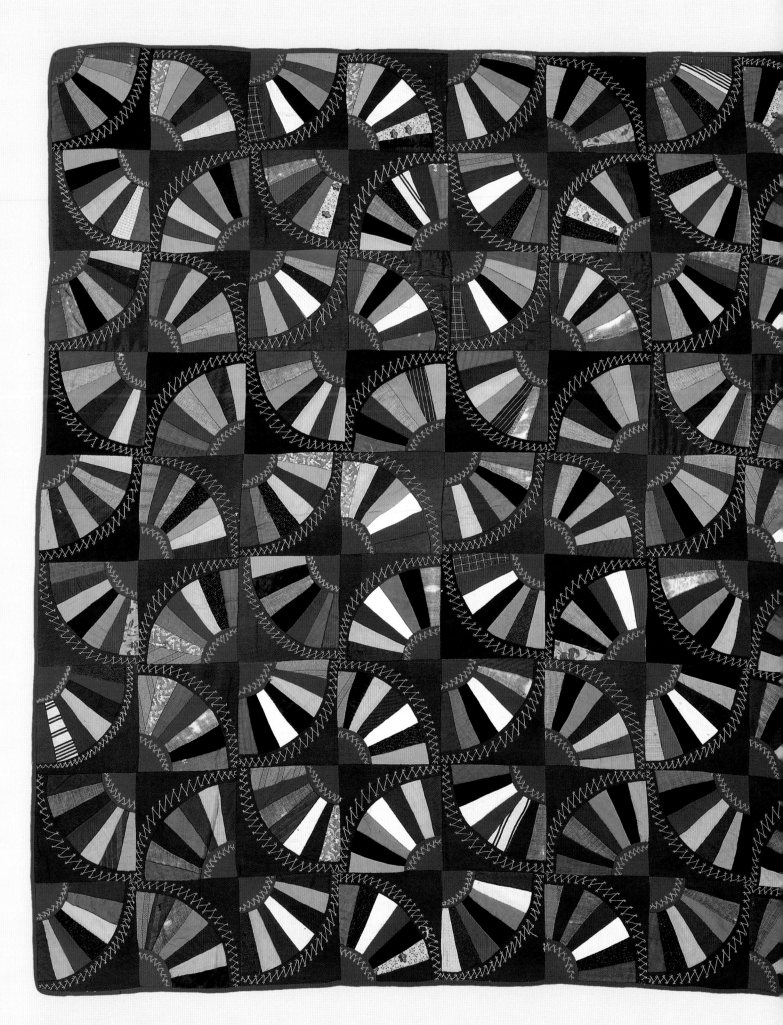

Fan

ELIZA VINCENT BRATTON

ca. 1895

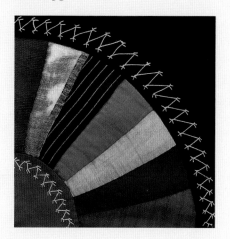

ELIZA Vincent Bratton was born in England in 1845 and immigrated to the United States around the age of sixteen. She made this Fan quilt of silk, wool, and cotton while living in Blackfoot City, a mining town northwest of Helena near present-day Ophir. Placer mining boomed around Blackfoot City in the 1860s and 1870s. Eliza's husband Hugh was one of the first miners to reach the area and amassed a small fortune there, but he died suddenly in 1881, leaving Eliza to raise their five children. Nearly one hundred years after the quilt was made circa 1895, Eliza's great-granddaughter Doreen Cook donated the quilt to the Montana Historical Society.

Mary Ronan, another miner's wife living in Blackfoot City in 1874, hinted in her memoir at how alienated a "respectable" married woman might feel in the mining town: "The 'city' was built where Ophir Gulch widens into meadowlands and rolling hills. It consisted of two rows of weather-beaten cabins, about thirty or forty rods in length, with a street between them. More of the cabins were saloons, gambling dens, and houses of ill fame than the homes of families."[15]

(above) Blackfoot City. (opposite) Fan, Eliza Vincent Bratton, ca. 1895, MHS *1996.63.01 (67" x 76", cotton, wool, silk, linen)*

Nine Patch, Millie Stine Talboys, 1898, MHQP 06-114-02 *(68" x 76", cotton)*

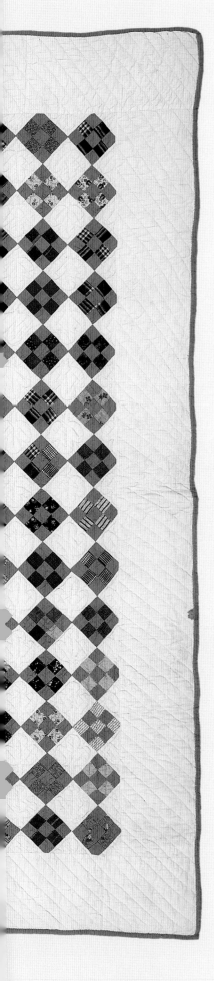

Nine Patch

MILLIE STINE TALBOYS
1898

MILLIE Stine Talboys made this Nine-Patch quilt for her sister Alice Stine Klumph in 1898. If the family's date for her quilt is correct, Millie developed excellent sewing skills at a very young age—she was only six years old in 1898.

At the time, the sisters were living in Missouri, but in May of that year, when Alice was two, the Stine family moved by covered wagon to Bozeman, Montana. A unique aspect of the Stines' westward journey is that they were able to make a visual record of it. In eastern Nebraska they met up with traveling photographer C. O. Corey, who carried his whole portrait studio—a camera, tripod, and developing and printing equipment—in his wagon. Millie later recalled: "Corey's wife had died and he had taken to the open road, hoping to find some comfort out in the open spaces. His six boys traveled with him as he went about taking family group pictures and photos of celebrations and other events." Millie remembers the cost being "only 25 cents for a good-sized photo," and so the Stines were able to purchase a lasting image of their overland journey.[16]

The family finally reached Bozeman in August, after a month's delay in Wyoming, where Millie's parents, Marion and Mollie, replenished their cash by working on a ranch. The family remained in Bozeman during the fall of 1898, but the next spring they moved to Fergus County, where Marion worked as a wagon freighter between Harlowton and Lewistown and Mollie worked in a hotel.

In this image of the Marion P. Stine family's covered wagon and C. O. Corey's "Portraits and Cabinet Work" wagon, Millie is on the wagon seat beside her mother, sister Alice is between her parents, and sister Thirza is riding the colt. Traveling photographer Corey is beside his wagon.

SISTERS Hester "Lyde" Ford and Mary Ford Weaver probably made this striking Snowflake quilt in Ohio in the 1890s. The two sisters were born in the small farm community of Fultonham Ohio—Mary in 1857 and Lyde in 1860. Their brother Jim moved to Kalispell in the late 1800s and built a hotel there in 1901. He then sent for his family—his brother Nels and Nels's wife Lettie, and his sisters Lyde and Mary—to come live with him in the hotel.

Jim developed properties, and Nels was a carpenter for the Kalispell Mercantile Company. In later years the family moved into a large house Jim built. The sisters continued quilting together in Montana, and Robert Ford, Nels and Lettie's grandson, remembers Mary and Lyde working on quilts in the living room when he was a small boy. He inherited the Snowflake quilt from his great-aunts.

HESTER "LYDE" FORD &
MARY FORD WEAVER

1890–1900

Lyde Ford, Don Ford (a relative from Ohio), Mary Weaver, Ludy Ford (also visiting)

Snowflake, Hester "Lyde" Ford and Mary Ford Weaver, 1890–1900,
MHQP 07-118-02 (58" x 76", cotton)

Sugan, possibly Lulu Bembrick, ca. 1900, MHQP 06-157-06 *(70" x 81", cotton, wool, velvet)*

Sugan

BECAUSE it evokes the state's romantic ranching past, perhaps no quilt type symbolizes Montana more perfectly than the sugan. Typically constructed from large squares of varying sizes and tied rather than quilted, sugans had the purely utilitarian purpose of keeping people warm. The word "sugan" is Irish in origin and was most heavily used in the Rocky Mountain region. In the eighteenth century, the term was used to describe "a straw mat used as a saddle blanket" but evolved in the early nineteenth century to mean a coarse woolen blanket.[17] Sugans are commonly associated with cowboys, but lumbermen also used the term for their bedding.

Marshall Bennett inherited this sugan from his grandmother Julia Bennett. Born in 1880 to Benjamin and Lulu Bembrick, Julia and her family came to Montana in 1864. Benjamin was first a buffalo hunter and then a rancher in the Crow Creek Valley near Radersburg. Around the turn of the century, Julia married Anson Bennett, also of Radersburg, but by 1930 the couple had divorced. Julia then started the Diamond J Ranch, a guest ranch near Ennis. Julia did not know how to sew, so she could not have made this sugan. The family guesses that it might instead have been made by Julia's mother Lulu.

Julia Bennett, who possibly inherited the quilt from her mother, and her son Donald B. Bennett, father of the current owner, ca. 1939

Charlie Scofield and Ord Ames prepare a bedroll with a pieced quilt, wool blankets, and a ground cloth. A sugan would have been more common in a bedroll.

Sugan, Anna Hildebrandt Burfening, 1900–1910, MHQP 31-12-03 *(62" x 85", wool)*

ANNA Hildebrandt Burfening made this sugan, most likely in the first decade of the twentieth century. The sugan traveled to Montana with Anna's son Edwin, who was born in Litchfield, Minnesota, in 1870. Edwin married Maude Caswell in Mananah, Minnesota, in 1893, and in 1915 the couple moved to Teton County, where they purchased the Cook Brothers cattle ranch west of Choteau. Although he split his time between Choteau and the Flathead Valley in his later years, Edwin managed the ranch until his death in 1959. Lucille Lussenden inherited her great-grandmother's sugan, and it is currently on loan to the Old Trail Museum in Choteau.

The border at the top of this sugan is known as a chin guard, whisker guard, or beard guard. Chin guards were added to keep the quilt from coming in contact with skin oils or mustache wax; they also made the quilt easier to care for because the owner could remove and wash the chin guard rather than washing the entire quilt.

ANNA HILDEBRANDT
BURFENING

1900–1910

Anna's son Edwin Burfening holding his great-granddaughter Karen (now McNutt), Karna Larson Burfening (Edwin's daughter-in-law—Lucille's mother), and Lucille Burfening Lussenden (Karen's mother), 1943–1944

Lucille, about age two, and Edwin Burfening in front of a log house on the ranch

Pineapple

JOHANNA Schmidt Stearns, wife of Prussian immigrant Henry Stearns, made this vibrant Pineapple Log Cabin quilt around the turn of the century in Russell Gulch, a mining camp in Colorado. Henry took up mining when the couple moved to Colorado around 1880, but in Prussia he had been a tailor. Henry and Johanna's daughter Bertha, who for a time worked as a dressmaker and milliner in nearby Central City, Colorado, recalled that she learned to sew from her father, although judging from this lovely quilt, Bertha's mother was a talented seamstress as well. Johanna pieced this quilt from fabric she obtained from Bertha's dressmaking business. Johanna likely had access to fine cloth because Bertha's clients included "ladies of the night" who could afford expensive taffetas.

Bertha married George Miller around 1909, and when the Millers moved to the Sarpy Creek area of Big Horn County in 1919, Bertha brought along several of her mother's quilts. A plain woolen sugan that Johanna made was featured in Kathlyn F. Sullivan's *Gatherings: America's Quilt Heritage*.

Edna Mae Miller, who married Bertha's son Edwin, recalls how she used to admire the Pineapple quilt: "Ed's mother never used it because it is such a heavy quilt and so pretty. We had a joke between the two of us, it was the only thing she owned and the only thing I wanted! (laughs) But I did want that quilt. So after she left the ranch and moved to town, I was cleaning house for her one day and she got the quilt out. We used to get it out and admire it and talk about it. I had never met Johanna. She died before Ed and I were married. But she used to talk about her, and we'd look at some of the things she'd done. That day Mom said to me, 'Well, since this is the only thing I have that you want, take it now.' And of course I did."[18]

Johanna Schmidt Stearns and her husband Henry Stearns, Central City, Colorado, ca. 1890

(opposite) *Pineapple, Johanna Schmidt Stearns, ca. 1900,* MHQP 22-13-07 *(74" x 83", satin, chintz)*

(left, from left to right) *Johanna Schmidt Stearns, friend and neighbor Dorothy Herman, and Bertha Stearns Miller on Miller homestead, 1928*

Crazy (above) and detail (right),
May Baxter Vestal, 1900–1905,
MHQP 47-12-01 (61" x 62", wool,
silk)

Crazy

MADE by May Baxter Vestal, a teacher in a one-room schoolhouse and the wife of a sheep rancher, this lovely, dark woolen Crazy quilt reflects the Two Dot area's sheep-ranching heritage.

May, born around 1873 to Harry and Maria Baxter, grew up on her parents' farm in Nelson, Pennsylvania. In the 1890s May moved to Montana, following her brother E. C. Baxter, who traveled west in 1893 and ultimately became a prominent Harlowton banker, rancher, and state legislator. May married Two Dot sheep rancher Clarence Bird "Bert" Vestal in 1899 and taught in a one-room country school southwest of Two Dot. A visitor to the Bear Creek School in 1906 "found a new frame building nicely furnished, and Mrs. Bert Vestal, one of the best teachers in the county teaching the school."[19]

May made this woolen Crazy quilt while she was living in Two Dot. The cloth in this quilt may have come from the nearby Big Timber woolen mill. Built in 1901, it was the state's first woolen mill. The fleece could easily have come from Two Dot, as the area's abundant grazing lands had attracted many sheep ranchers at the turn of the century.

May's nieces Frances Marie Baxter and Helen Elizabeth Baxter, the current owner's mother, at about ages nine and five, ca. 1905

Mary Mollander, the quilt's current owner, remembers her grandfather using her great-aunt May's quilt as a lap blanket in the 1940s. Nobody else in her family showed much interest in the quilt, preferring the more colorful silk quilts like the one made by the Two Dot Ladies Aid in 1905 and pictured on this page. This silk Crazy quilt was acquired by Don Martin at a church raffle and remains with the Martin family of Two Dot.

Woolen Crazy quilts, though perhaps not as glamorous as their silk and velvet Victorian counterparts, do have a certain charm. "I think of these wool Crazy quilts as more of a vernacular tradition; many of them show signs of wear, which most fine silk Crazy parlor throws do not," quilt historian Janet Berlo writes. "Though sharing many characteristics with silk Crazy quilts, they were intended as utility quilts— albeit ones on which much attention was lavished."[20]

Crazy, Two Dot Ladies Aid, 1905, MHQP 47-11-03 (71" x 93", cotton, wool, silk). The silks in this quilt are more common in the Crazy quilt genre than the wools of May Baxter Vestal's quilt.

Crazy, women at the Mayflower Mine, 1901, MHQP 51-01-01 (68" x 79", *silk, satin, velvet, flannel, corduroy*)

Crazy

THIS Crazy quilt was made by women at the Mayflower Mine, which the *Anaconda Standard* at one point dubbed "one of the richest ever in the state." Located near Whitehall in the Tobacco Root Mountains, the Mayflower was discovered by miners from Butte in 1896. The *Standard* recounted the tale of the mine's discovery: "[I]t has been said that when the first specimen of rock came from the Mayflower to [a Butte assayer's] office, he scornfully told the prospector that he could get no value from the country rock. 'Assay it anyway,' said the prospector. 'Here's your fee.' The assay showed a value of $1,000 to the ton."[21]

The mine was later sold to William A. Clark. Because Clark never disclosed how much the mine produced, rumors abounded about the Mayflower Mine's riches, and "there is a story to the effect that millions were taken from the property." The story may not be far off. The Mayflower was extremely productive through 1905, and in its first ten years the mine is estimated to have produced as much as $3 million in silver and gold ore.[22]

This quilt, thought to have been made at the community's boardinghouse, was a group effort for the women at the Mayflower. It contains signatures of over twenty families who were living at the mine in 1901. The center block contains an embroidered representation of the mine entrance, with the word "Mayflower" over the door and the date beneath.

Mayflower Mine southeast of Whitehall

Raymond A. Pratz   Dr. E. E. Edmonson   Wadsworth

...nal Laundry   F. O. E. Co.   C. H. Campbell   Mr & Mrs
                                                                       F. N. Major

Louis K. Hammars   Woodman of the   Margarethe
                                    World   Lodge
                                    Great Falls Camp   No 9
                                    No 67

                              May A. Flaherty

...s Irving Duncan   Lee M. Ford   George Scrivens

John Duncan   Metal Trades Council   Evelyn   Building Trades
                               of   Council
                               Great Falls   of
                               Montana   Great Falls
                                                                             Montana

                                                                                        Mrs. D...

Order of   Great Falls
Moose   Dairy Products
Falls, No 532   Arthur   Malmberg   Clarence   Co.

Retail Clerk's   F. O. ...
Union
No 57   Electricians   Mystic Rebekah
               Local   Victor   Lodge No 20
               No 121
               Great Falls   Knights of Pythias
Scandinavian
Fraternity   Woodmen Circle   Cataract Lodge
Great Falls   Maybloom   No 18
No 2   Grove No 109

Sons of Norman   Knights of   A. F. O. M.
...iend   Bismarck   Columbus   Great Falls
                       Lodge   Great Falls Council No 365
                       No 1   No 1593   N...

Red Cross

DURING World War I, the American Red Cross encouraged women to contribute to the war effort by quilting. Women throughout the country raised money for the organization, which was founded in 1881 by Clara Barton, by selling spaces for signatures on Red Cross–themed quilts. Often the finished quilts were then auctioned, generating additional funds.

The Cascade County Ladies Auxiliary to the Order of the United Commercial Traveler (UCT), a fraternal benefit society founded by traveling salesmen at the end of the nineteenth century, made this Red Cross quilt in 1918. The small spaces most likely sold for around twenty-five cents, but the large cross in the center may have raised as much as one hundred dollars. After raffling the quilt in April 1918, the Ladies Auxiliary was able to donate $1,060.80 to the Red Cross.

Red Cross volunteers and sailors at the Helena train depot, ca. 1917

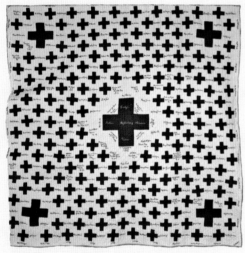

(opposite and above) Red Cross, UCT Ladies Auxiliary, 1918, MHS XI982.71.01 *(81" x 82", cotton)*

(right) reverse side

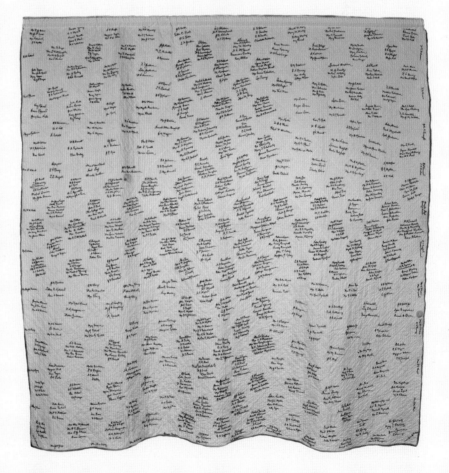

Red Cross, Big Timber Lutheran Ladies Aid, 1918–1922, MHQP 40-04-03 *(60" x 74", cotton)*

Red Cross

BY the fall of 1918, the war in Europe was not the only pressing problem addressed by the Red Cross. That September an influenza epidemic swept the globe, and by June 1919, 675,000 Americans had died from the disease. The Red Cross responded to the crisis by creating a National Committee on Influenza and mobilizing professionals and volunteers to fill the void left by American doctors and nurses who were working overseas. The Red Cross's role in combating the pandemic heightened the need for the fund-raising efforts already undertaken by the country's quilters.

This Red Cross quilt made by the women of the Big Timber Lutheran Ladies Aid contains one very famous name. Around the second cross from the left in the fifth row these words appear: "Woodrow Wilson passed through Big Timber September 11, 1919." Wilson did indeed pass through Big Timber that day. He traveled first to Billings and then to Helena as part of a nationwide speaking tour to drum up support for American involvement in the League of Nations. His train stopped briefly in Livingston, about thirty miles east of Big Timber. The *Helena Daily Independent* reported: "It was expected the president would speak 10 minutes at Livingston, but the crowd was so dense, the cheering so continuous and the excitement so great that the train pulled out before the great crowd was quiet enough to have heard the president had he started to speak."[23] It is unclear if Wilson actually signed the quilt square, but it would not have been unprecedented. Today the American Red Cross has its own collection of Red Cross quilts, and among them are quilts signed by Theodore Roosevelt and Woodrow Wilson.

This illustration of Red Cross volunteers marching in a parade appeared in Yellowstone County Montana in the World War, 1917–1919, *edited by W. W. Gail and published in Billings in 1919.*

RED CROSS

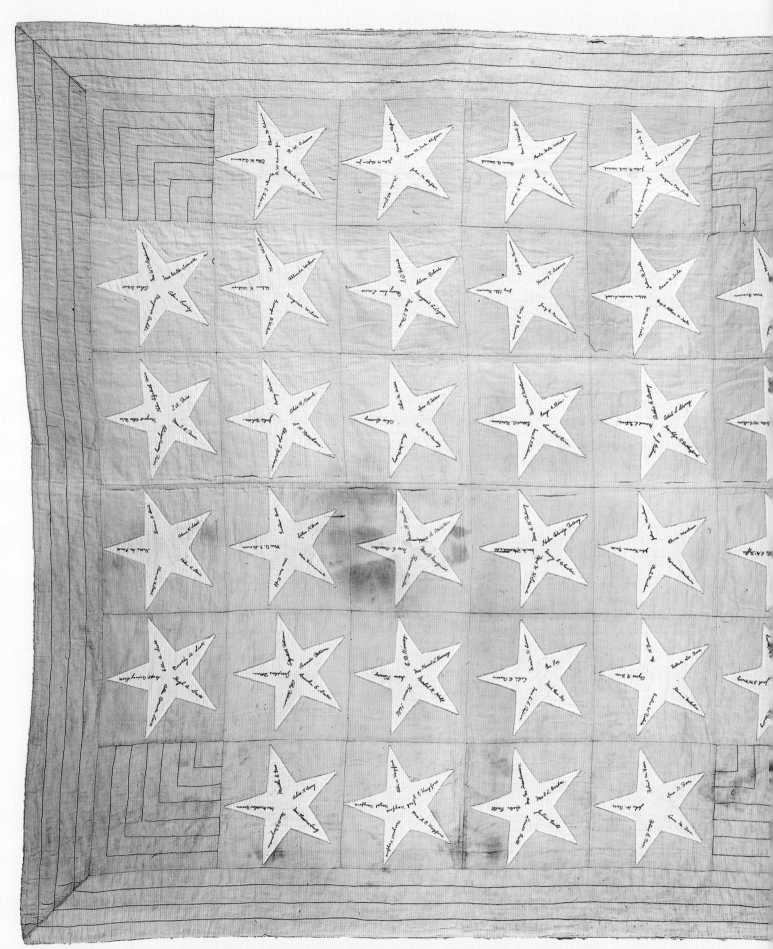

Star Signature, members of the Missoula First Presbyterian Church, ca. 1919, MHQP 04-68-05 (75" x 76", cotton)

THIS elegant Star Signature quilt—featuring the signatures of several famous Missoulians—was nearly lost to Missoula's First Presbyterian Church in 1991. The church was cleaning house, and this quilt had been placed in the rummage sale. Fortunately, Gloria Anderson recognized several names stitched into the stars and understood that the quilt offered a unique glimpse into Missoula's history.

One of the stars belonged to A. J. Gibson, one of Missoula's most respected turn-of-the-century architects, and his family. Gibson designed several buildings on the University of Montana campus, Missoula's Carnegie library, the county courthouse, and numerous homes and row houses. In 1915 Gibson came out of retirement to design the First Presbyterian Church.

The signatures of several members of the John R. Toole family also appear on the quilt. An early Missoula politician and industrialist, John participated in the 1889 Montana constitutional convention, served in the state legislature, and eventually became president of the Blackfoot Milling Company at Bonner. Toole's grandson Kenneth Ross Toole became one of Montana's most famous and influential

One of the quilt's makers was church member Jenny Thomas.

First Presbyterian Church, Missoula, 1918

historians. K. Ross Toole's parents also had a star, but they included only the name of their oldest son John Howard Toole Jr., who was born in 1918. Since K. Ross was born in 1920, it seems likely that the quilt was made during the period between their births.

The quilt also includes the names of the pastor of the First Presbyterian Church, Reverend John Maclean, and his family. At the time the quilt was made, the pastor's eldest son Norman was probably working in a logging camp for the U.S. Forest Service. Later, however, Norman Maclean wrote *A River Runs Through It,* a collection of stories about growing up as a pastor's son in Montana. He became one of the state's most beloved authors.

Album Block, Clarissa "Clara" Plum Sanguine, 1919, MHQP 07-287-01 *(61" x 78", cotton)*

CLARISSA "CLARA" PLUM
SANGUINE

1919

LIKE many Montana women, Clarissa "Clara" Sanguine was inspired to contribute to the war effort. Instead of making bright red crosses, however, Clara used the Christian Cross or Album Block pattern, which became a popular pattern for signature quilts in the second half of the nineteenth century.

To raise money, Clara charged ten cents for each signature and then sold the finished quilt in a local raffle. The man who won the raffle returned the quilt to Clara. The next year, with the community's blessing, she auctioned it off again, and once more, the winner returned the quilt to Clara, allowing her to keep it in the family. According to Clara's grandson, the quilt won a first-place ribbon in the 1932 Havre fair.

Clara, her husband William, and her son Russell had moved from Ontario, Canada, to Cottonwood, a small community in northern Hill County, Montana, where William and Russell farmed in the spring and summer and mined coal in the winter. A local history noted that Clara was "well known for her beautiful hooked rugs, her quilts, and her paintings."[24]

Clarissa and William H. Sanguine (right) with (from left) their daughter-in-law Daisy Webster Sanguine (wife of Russell) and sons Leonard and Russell, north of Havre in the Simpson-Cottonwood area in 1918

CHAPTER THREE

Hard Times | 1920 TO 1939

*H*ard times came to Montana's plains well before the stock market crash of 1929 sparked the Great Depression. Many of the state's woes in this period can be traced to the drought that struck Montana's farmers in 1917, just as the United States' entry into World War I caused commodities prices to skyrocket. At first the drought's effects were felt mainly along the High Line, but from 1919 onward the lack of rainfall affected the entire state. The dry weather ushered in forest fires, hungry gophers, swarms of locusts, and dust storms similar to those on the Southern Plains a decade later. Exacerbating these hardships was the nationwide recession at the conclusion of World War I, which hit Montana especially hard. For farmers, peacetime meant an end to the European demand for wheat and the federal price controls that had kept profits high. The war's end also decreased the demand for raw materials, and Montana towns dependent on the mining and lumber industries faced shutdowns and unemployment.

Tumbling Blocks, quiltmaker unknown, ca. 1920, MHS 2001.68.01, MHQP 05-28-01 (detail, pieced, 74" x 84", cotton)

Fence covered by soil drift, Two Triangles Farm, northeastern Montana, ca. 1920

Thus the Roaring Twenties, so prosperous elsewhere, were a decade of despair for many Montanans. Between 1919 and 1925, banks foreclosed on twenty thousand mortgages. As farmers defaulted on their debts, the banks that had lent money failed as well. In all, over one-half of the state's commercial banks closed their doors, and many Montana families lost their life savings. The effect of this downturn was to reverse the population influx of previous years. As many as sixty thousand people, primarily from rural areas, left Montana. These stories—of bankruptcy, bank closures, and outward migration—are familiar to students of the Great Depression. But it is notable that Montanans faced these problems at least ten years before the federal government began its efforts to right the economy.

With the onset of the Great Depression in the early thirties, conditions continued to deteriorate. Copper prices plummeted, as did the value of Anaconda Copper Mining Company stock. Thousands of workers in Butte, Anaconda, Great Falls, and East Helena lost their jobs when the industry cut back on production. Montanans were desperate, and as historian Mary Murphy points out, "It was only in these dire straits that people turned to the government, and they did not ask for charity but for work."[1]

Although historians debate whether Franklin Delano Roosevelt's New Deal programs successfully ended the Depression, they certainly helped thousands of Montana men and women. Per capita, Montana received more New Deal money than any other state but one. The Agricultural Adjustment Administration paid millions to farmers who agreed to reduce acreage under cultivation. The Farm Credit Administration helped ranchers and farmers avoid foreclosure by refinancing with low-interest loans. The Civilian Conservation Corps employed thousands of young men to fight fires, build roads, and plant trees in Montana's forests. The construction of the Fort Peck Dam—by far the largest work project in Montana—employed more than ten thousand workers at its peak.

Some programs, such as those carried out by the Works Progress Administration, offered work relief to women. In addition to its many public improvement projects, the WPA sponsored twenty-three sewing rooms in Montana—five of which were on Indian reservations. The women who worked in these sewing rooms produced garments and household goods for people on relief. However, this economic help did not come without strings, as these women were required to wear ugly, shapeless uniforms, which signified to their neighbors that they were on relief. "They were good sewers and made nice clothing and flannel sleep wear for distribution to needy people," recalled Julia Trees, whose mother had worked in a WPA sewing room. "They didn't mind the eight hour days bent over a machine but never should they have been singled out in this way with uniforms."[2]

Fort Peck Dam workers, 1936

Two Medicine WPA sewing club, Blackfeet Reservation, 1930s. Left to right: Mrs. Calf Looking, Mae Williamson, Nora Spanish, Louise Pepion, Tiny Racine, Anna Potts, Rosy Big Beaver

Women like Julia's mother sewed for a living, but in the midst of the Great Depression, women were also stitching for pleasure. Indeed, by the 1930s, a national quilting revival was in full swing. This resurgence had its roots in women's quilt-making efforts during World War I, but it was also fed by another earlier trend—a fascination with America's colonial past that, in the first decades of the twentieth century, sparked interest in women's traditional handcrafts, especially quilts. The country's first "quilt historians," women such as Ruth Finley, Carrie Hall, Rose Kretsinger, and Marie Webster, studied and disseminated historic quilt patterns. Webster, whose book, *Quilts: Their Story and How to Make Them* was published in 1915, explicitly linked patchwork to patriotism, writing that the quiltmaking trend "should be a source of much satisfaction to all patriotic Americans who believe that the true source of our nation's strength lies in keeping the family hearth flame bright."[3]

As historians of the colonial era, these women were not always reliable. Most of the patterns they associated with that time period actually developed in the nineteenth century, as many eighteenth-century women had neither the time nor the resources to quilt. Nevertheless, these authors got American women interested in quilting again. Marie Webster was particularly influential in this regard. One of the first quilt entrepreneurs, Webster designed patterns for *Ladies' Home Journal* and sold her patterns and kits through her Practical Patchwork

Children napping at WPA nursery school, ca. 1938

Needlecraft
Magazine,
September 1928

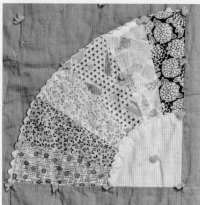

Grandmother's Fan (shown above; detail at left). The quilt was made by the women of Benchland for Nell Torrison, ca. 1930 (MHS 2008.02.01) Made of cotton cloth, the pieced quilt measures 69" x 80".

Company. (One of Webster's patterns, Windblown Tulips, appears in Chapter 4.) Soon other quilt entrepreneurs followed Webster's lead. By the 1920s and 1930s, quilt patterns were being published in newspapers around the country, and myriad mail-order catalogs offered women access to the quilt kits and patterns.

With the sale of quilting books, patterns, and kits occurring on a national level by the 1920s and 1930s, the homogenizing trend in quiltmaking that had started at the turn of the century accelerated. Now we look back at the increasing uniformity in quilting and mourn the loss of regionalism and originality, but, as quilt scholars Anne Copeland and Beverly Dunivent point out, there was a reason quilt kits were so popular: "Kits represented twentieth-century technology during a time in our culture when the assembly line was popular and there was little prejudice against repetitiveness."[4]

Even as the Great Depression deepened and quiltmaking became less affordable, the number of women stitching quilts grew. Quilt historians speculate that quilts fulfilled the psychological needs of discouraged Americans, associated as they were with maternal warmth and protection. The cheery pastel quilts so popular in the 1930s seem to reflect a desire to break from the dreariness of the times and to express hope for the future. Reverting to traditional folk arts was a way for women to express their link to romanticized pioneer-era women who worked determinedly and overcame hardship and loneliness. Quiltmaking also offered women an escape from the difficulties of the present and a way to bring pleasure into their lives.

The Montana Historic Quilt Project uncovered numerous quilts made during the Depression, especially standard favorites like Grandmother's Flower Garden, Dresden Plate, and Double Wedding Ring. Perhaps this abundance of quilts from the 1920s and 1930s simply reflects Montana quilters' participation in the national quilting revival. Perhaps it is a reflection of the fact that Montana's hard times were longer and deeper than those in other parts of the nation, heightening the need for the symbolic comfort quilts offered. But perhaps the reason so many of these Depression quilts are still around is that Montanans want to remember what their families went through as the promise of the Northern Plains slowly slipped from their grasp. ❖

(opposite) Flower Basket, Mary Dean Flaherty, 1920–1929, MHS 1983.40.02 (detail, appliquéd, 75" x 78", linen).

Pineapple

EMMA LOUISE RILEY
SMITH

ca. 1920

EMMA Louise Riley Smith made this vibrant Pineapple appliqué quilt. Born to James Wesley Riley, a farmer and former slave, in Arkansas in 1881, Emma moved with her family to Liberia when she was fourteen, fulfilling her great-grandfather's long-standing wish for the family to "return to Africa."[5] Emma lived in Liberia for fifteen years, but after her brother and parents had died, she yearned to see her American family. Accompanied by her younger sister Thelma, who had been born in Liberia, Emma moved back to the United States around 1910 or 1912. She spent some time with relatives in Arkansas before eventually making her way to Butte, where she married Martin Luther Smith in 1913. Later, the family moved to Lewistown, where Emma earned money as a laundress and Martin worked as a cook for the Milwaukee Road. Then the family moved again, this time to Great Falls, where Martin worked as a cook for the Great Northern Railroad.

As an African American woman, Emma was certainly in the minority in Montana, but a few small, thriving urban black communities had begun to develop in the state around the turn of the century. Helena, in fact, boasted the second-oldest black community in the Pacific Northwest. The mining boom that began in 1864 drew the first African Americans to the city, and by the 1890s Helena had black-owned barber shops, a grocery store, and a saloon as well as black churches, fraternal groups, and a women's benevolent association. Although not all black communities were as large as Helena's, Butte and Great Falls also had African American churches, and Kalispell, Butte, Anaconda, Billings, and Bozeman had black women's clubs.

In Great Falls, Emma was an active member of the African American Union Bethel Church, where she served as conference secretary for the church's board of trustees and president of the Women's Missionary Mite Society. Emma was a prolific and talented quilter and often raffled her quilts as part of her exhaustive fund-raising for the society. Her daughter Lucille Thompson registered fourteen of her quilts with the Montana Historic Quilt Project.

Emma's graceful Carolina Lily quilt, pictured on this page, is of special historic significance. Emma started the quilt while still living in Liberia and finished it after she moved to Montana.

(opposite) Pineapple, Emma Louise Riley Smith, ca. 1920, MHQP 06-103-09 (72" x 94", cotton)

(right) Emma Louise Riley Smith with her daughters (left to right) Madeline Smith (Haskins Clark), Lucille W. Smith (Thompson), and Alma Smith (Jacobs)

(above right) Carolina Lily, Emma Louise Riley Smith, ca. 1920, MHS 1995.84.06 (pieced and appliquéd, 72" x 78", cotton)

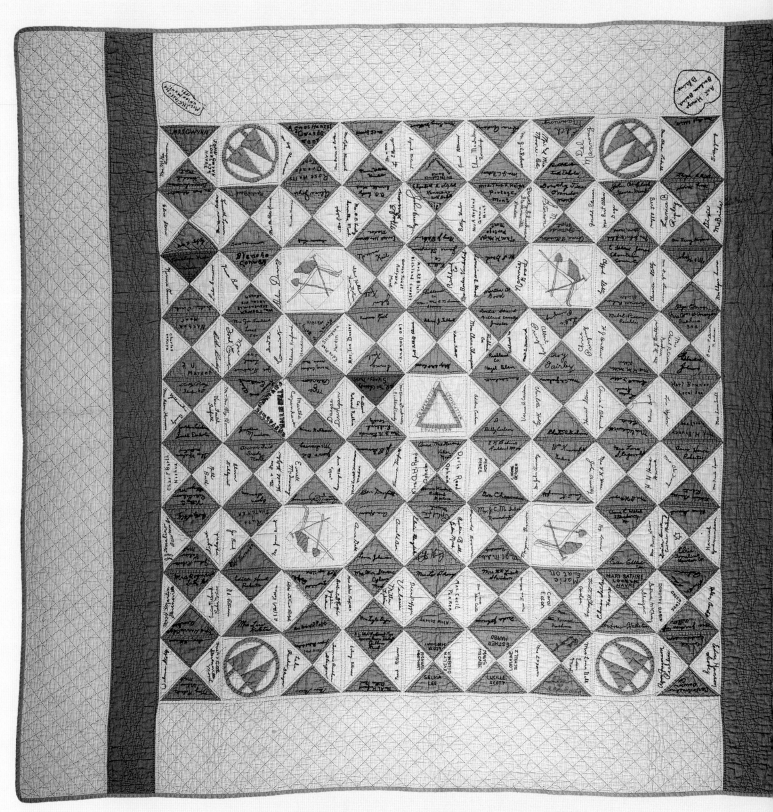

Patchwork Signature, women of the Montana and North Dakota Farmers Union,
1920, MHQP 24-04-02 (72" x 81", cotton)

Patchwork Signature

MADE by the women of the Montana and North Dakota Farmers Union—a grassroots organization founded in 1902 to help small farmers—the spaces for signatures on this patchwork quilt were sold to raise money so that women and children could participate more fully in the organization. Besides containing myriad signatures, including some added in later years, the quilt features several symbols dear to the organization. A plow, a rake, and a hoe appear on one block. Another contains a triangle with the three modes of action advocated by the Farmers Union: cooperation, legislation, and education.

The Farmers Union began organizing in Montana in 1912, and membership soared in the 1920s as its populist message resounded with farmers facing difficult times. Both men and women joined the Montana Farmers Union, but they did not always enjoy equal status. In her 1956 history, Mildred K. Stoltz, longtime education director of the Montana Farmers Union, quoted a 1926 letter from the male editor of the *Montana Union Farmer*, which urged the organization to become more inclusive of women: "Agriculture does not agree with those who are proclaiming the failure of equal suffrage because the women have not, in a few years, through the use of the ballot, introduced the millennium. We believe they have done remarkably well—in fact, quite as well as the male portion of the voting population. . . . Many a man has risen by the impetus and inspiration given by his wife and family. They have been compelled to take a bigger view point, to make a bigger exertion, in order to provide a safe future. . . . For that same purpose, why not enlist the efforts of the women in widening the influence of the union? By taking the women and children into the Union's activities the Union will make for itself the place in our state which its principles and ambitions deserve."[6]

Barbara Baird Varner (Hauge), who was last to inherit the quilt, gave it to the Montana Farmers Union.

Writing thirty years later, however, Stoltz reported little progress: "The opinions sounded in 1926 should be applauded and it would be most gratifying to be able to record success in this endeavor, but it will be many more years before equality of sexes is reached in any bracket of the Farmers Union."[7]

For her contributions to the organization, Mildred was given this signature quilt. Loraine Schultz Coe inherited the quilt from Mildred, and when Loraine died, she left the quilt to Barbara Hauge of Turner, another longtime Farmers Union activist.

Mildred Stoltz (seated far left) at a Farmers Union meeting

Grandmother's Flower Garden

AUDREY MANLEY &
ANNE ARNESON STEVENS

finished early 1980s

IN the mid-1920s, while she was living on a farm north of Poplar on the Fort Peck Reservation, Audrey Manley cut all the hexagons for this colorful Grandmother's Flower Garden quilt (opposite) and began piecing the top. Eventually, Audrey gave the unfinished top and remaining pieces to Anne Arneson Stevens, also of Poplar, and in the early 1980s Anne finished piecing the top as a gift for her daughter Doris Pascal, who now lives in Great Falls. The hand-quilting was done by a group of Assiniboine and Sioux women who belonged to a local quilting club. Rather than following the hexagons, the women quilted in the shell design often preferred by Plains Indian quilters.

Along with Dresden Plates and Double Wedding Rings, Grandmother's Flower Gardens were among the most popular Depression-era quilts. The pattern has its roots in nineteenth-century hexagon quilts. Also known as Mosaic or Honeycomb quilts, hexagon patchwork quilts were popular throughout the nineteenth century because they easily adapted to changing fabric trends. According to Barbara Brackman, the hexagon quilt went from "chintz to silk to wool to calicoes, first in brown cottons, then grays and then pastels."[8]

Although the hexagons could be arranged in a variety of patterns, by the 1920s quilters preferred the Grandmother's Flower Garden arrangement, where a center hexagon was surrounded rings of hexagon "petals." The quilt top pictured on this page was rescued from a dumpster in Billings; it follows the basic Grandmother's Flower Garden arrangement but contains fabrics dating from the 1830s to the 1870s.

Audrey Manley, 1951, Poplar

Anne Stevens, 1997, Poplar

(opposite) Grandmother's Flower Garden, Audrey Manley and Anne Arneson Stevens, finished early 1980s, MHQP 02-97-01 *(75" x 96", cotton)*

(above) Grandmother's Flower Garden quilt top, quiltmaker unknown, 1830–1870, MHQP 22-133-11 *(63" x 67", silk), with fabrics dating 1830s–1870s.*

MARY EDWARDS &
JOHANNA GILBERTSON

1926

SISTERS Mary Edwards and Johanna Gilbertson of Kalispell made this pieced Nosegay quilt as a wedding gift for Johanna's daughter Mabel, who married Byron O'Neil in 1926. The wedding quilt must have been good luck for the couple—they marked their fiftieth wedding anniversary in 1976. The *Kalispell Daily Interlake* reported on the celebration thrown by the O'Neils' children and grandchildren: "Two hundred guests signed the guest book. The serving table was decorated with an arrangement of trailing greenery, gold roses, and white chrysanthemums surrounding the three-tiered anniversary cake. On the guest book table was a gold-framed wedding announcement."[9] Quilting seems to have been a skill the women of the O'Neil family passed on to future generations. Serving cake at the reception was Byron's cousin Wilda May O'Neil Wilson, whose Noah's Ark baby quilt appears later in this chapter.

Also known as Bride's Bouquet, the Nosegay pattern became popular in the 1930s. The Old Chelsea Station Needlecraft Service, a mail-order company based in New York, attributed the pattern to Laura Wheeler. It sold the pattern for the attractive low price of ten cents.

(above) Johanna Gilbertson

(opposite) Nosegay, Mary Edwards and Johanna Gilbertson, 1926, MHQP 07-112-03 *(80" x 94", cotton)*

Mary Edwards, standing beside her husband Bill on porch, and their daughter Mabel (on step), for whom the quilt was made

OLIVE White Nixon of Augusta carefully stuffed each tiny grape to add dimension to this graceful appliqué quilt, which most likely was based on a Mountain Mist pattern.

Born in Minnesota in 1863 to Silvanus and Charlotte Nicholson White, Olive experienced a dramatic frontier childhood, as noted in her obituary: "She lived through the early Indian massacre in Minnesota. She and other family members were driven from their home by Indians, but escaped to the stockade at Sauk Center. The father, Sylvanus White, was in the Civil War at the time and for several years was unable to learn the whereabouts of his family. After locating the family, he came with them to Montana in a covered wagon from Oklahoma."[10]

In 1883 Olivia married John Nixon, who was born in England but moved in 1851 to Canada to join the Mounted Police. Then, in 1873, he moved to Sun River, Montana, where he ran a livery stable and way station for freight wagons moving between Helena and Fort Benton. Here John played a small but crucial role in Montana's early transportation history: "He carried the late J. J. Hill and Colonel Broadwater in one of his stage coaches from Sun River to Helena, when they were scouting for a route for the Montana Central railroad, now a part of the Great Northern System."[11]

Olive helped John run the livery business until 1888, when the Nixons moved to the Augusta area and established a cattle ranch near the headwaters of the Sun River. Olive died in Augusta in 1951, and her quilt is now owned by her grandson R. J. Weisner.

Martha's Vineyard

OLIVE WHITE NIXON

ca. 1926

Olive White Nixon and grandchild, ca. 1920

(opposite) *Martha's Vineyard, Olive White Nixon, ca. 1926,* MHQP 02-02-02 *(detail, 74" x 84", cotton)*
(above) *The Nixon ranch, near Augusta, was homesteaded in 1888. The ranch house is pictured ca. 1940.*

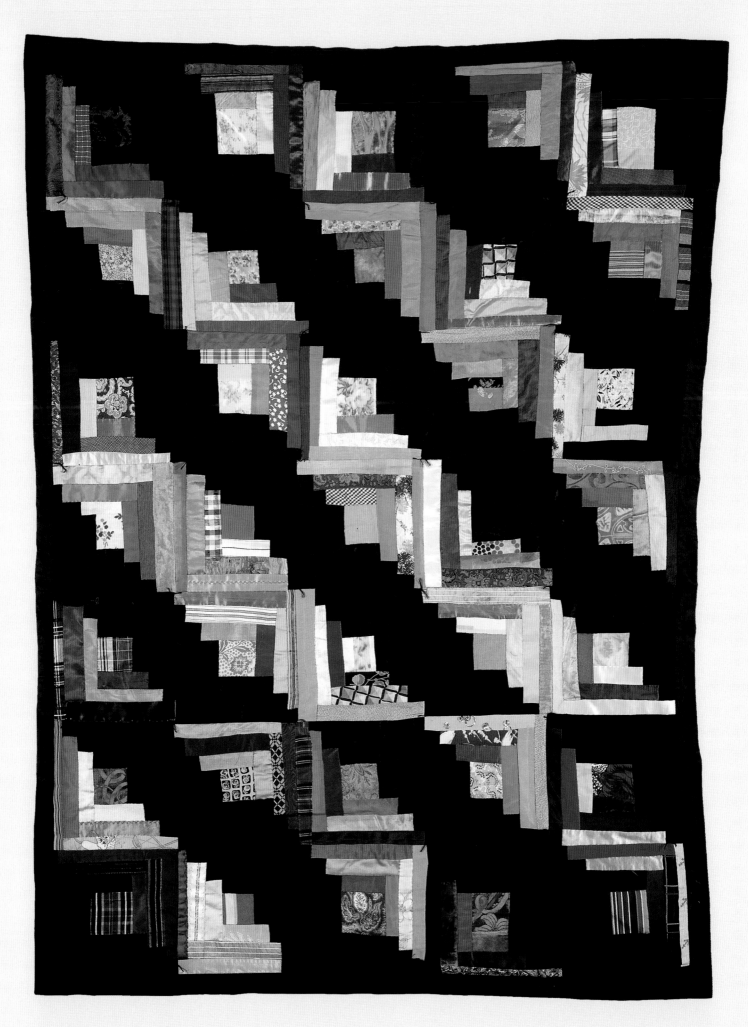

VEVA Marks Smith of Townsend made this Log Cabin quilt from the scraps of her family's old clothing. When she put together the blocks for the quilt, Veva chose the Straight Furrows design. Given her busy life, it is perhaps no surprise that she was only able to complete the quilt top. The quilt was finished in the late 1990s by Mary Lou Hanson of Butte.

Born in 1878 on a ranch near Townsend, Veva was the daughter of an enterprising father—in addition to ranching, J. R. Marks owned a bakery and several freighting lines. In 1903 Veva married Charles Wolf Smith, who had come to Broadwater County three years earlier to teach school. At the urging of his wife, Charles went to Ohio to complete his medical education while Veva and their young daughter Veva Alice remained in Montana. When Charles returned, the family moved to the gold-mining town of Kendall in Fergus County so the doctor could operate the hospital there. He was later chosen to represent the county in the state legislature.

Because Townsend was closer to the state capital, the family moved back to Veva's hometown, where Dr. Nixon began practicing medicine and Veva took over the operation of her father's ranch after he suffered a stroke in 1908. Charles died in the influenza epidemic of 1918–1919. Veva continued running her family's ranch until she was almost ninety.

For Veva, quiltmaking was a family affair. She also worked on the baby quilt pictured on this page with her mother Mary Frost Marks and her daughters Veva Alice Smith MacLeod, Mary Bill Smith Kavanaugh, and Alvena Smith Hooper. Well loved for many years, this quilt was also repaired by Mary Lou Hanson.

Veva Marks Smith, center, with her daughters (left) Veva Alice Smith (MacLeod) and Alvena Smith (Hooper), ca. 1925

Veva's mother Mary Frost Marks

Veva's daughters (left to right) Mary Bill Smith (Kavanaugh), Veva Alice, and Alvena, ca. 1920

(opposite) Log Cabin, Veva Marks Smith, 1920s, MHQP 43-21-02 (51" x 69", cotton, silk)

(above) Block quilt, Veva Marks Smith and her mother and daughters, 1920s, MHQP 43-21-03 (47" x 48", satin, taffeta)

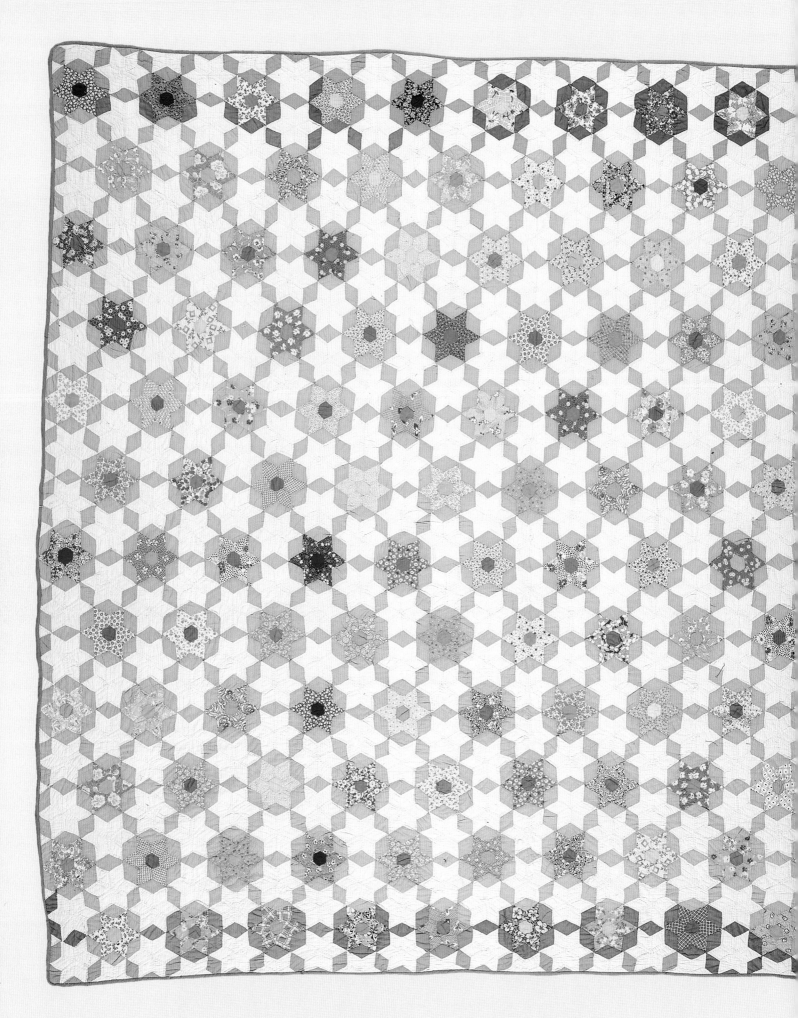

Star Bouquet

NETTIE OSSETTE
STERNER MINER

1920S

OSSETTE Miner pieced the top for this Star Bouquet quilt herself but quilted it with the help of several neighbor women. Born in Hope, Kansas, in 1889, Ossette and her husband Fay moved to Montana from Davenport, Nebraska, in 1915 and settled in the southwestern corner of what is now Daniels County in northeastern Montana, an area on the Fort Peck Reservation opened to white homesteaders by the Congressional Act of May 30, 1908. The small community near the Miners' homestead took its name from Ossette, who acted as the postmistress from 1917 to 1936 and also served as the local midwife.

Throughout the 1930s, the Ossette Quilters gathered together to quilt. Ossette's daughter Marjorie Miner Solberg recalls the get-togethers of her childhood as community affairs: "Quilt tops were pieced and the neighborhood was invited to a big dinner and hours of quilting and visiting. The men played cards and discussed farming. Older children were in school, little ones came to the party, and babies were passed around and loved."[12]

The women of Ossette also made a friendship quilt (detail pictured on this page) as a gift for Myrtle Baird, who lived with her husband Edwin on a farm near the Miners. Ossette, Kathleen Baird, Gertrude Waitschies, Maude Heeter, Selma Hallower, Serene Foss, Edna Hallower, Borghild Trang, Anna Trang, Berniece Foss, and Marjorie Miner each made blocks with their names embroidered in the center. The women then gathered to arrange and join the blocks and hand-quilt the gift. Myrtle's friendship quilt was later given to Marjorie Solberg, who donated it to the Daniels County Museum and Pioneer Town in Scobey.

Ossette Miner and her husband Fay

Ossette family homestead, home of the Ossette post office 1917–1936

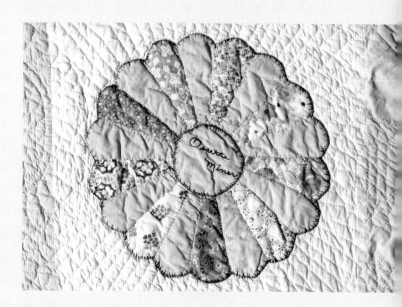

(left) Star Bouquet, Nettie Ossette Sterner Miner, 1920s, MHQP 37-02-02 (78" x 81", cotton)

(right) Friendship quilt, Ossette Quilters, 1930s, MHQP 37-01-01 (detail, 62" x 84", cotton)

LIZZIE Borho Williams's Double Wedding Ring quilt, with its remarkable circularity and interlocking rings, is a masterpiece of design and skill. Lizzie made the quilt with the help of her husband Elmer, who designed this inter-locking variation on the standard Double Wedding Ring. Lizzie, who was born in 1887 in the town of Stearns, near Wolf Creek, lived with Elmer in Great Falls, where the couple owned a saloon and she worked as a laundress. Lizzie loved making quilts and sometimes invited friends to stitch with her, although it is unknown whether anyone helped her quilt this Double Wedding Ring.

Enormously popular in the 1930s, the Double Wedding Ring pattern showcased the skills of "virtuoso quilter makers," according to quilt historian Kari Ronning, and "many depression-era quiltmakers took on their challenge to keep their minds off their troubles."[13] The name of the quilt also attracted quiltmakers who wanted to commemorate marital bliss.

LIZZIE BORHO WILLIAMS

late 1920s

Lizzie Borho Williams,
ca. 1940s

Elmer J. Williams, 1911

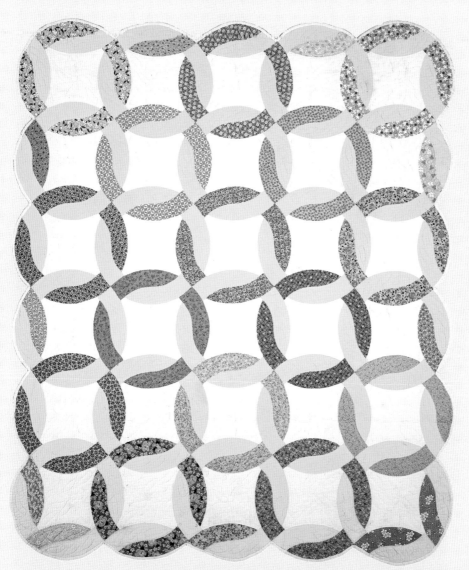

Interlocking Double Wedding Ring, Lizzie Borho Williams, late 1920s, MHQP 06-138-01
(67" x 82", cotton)

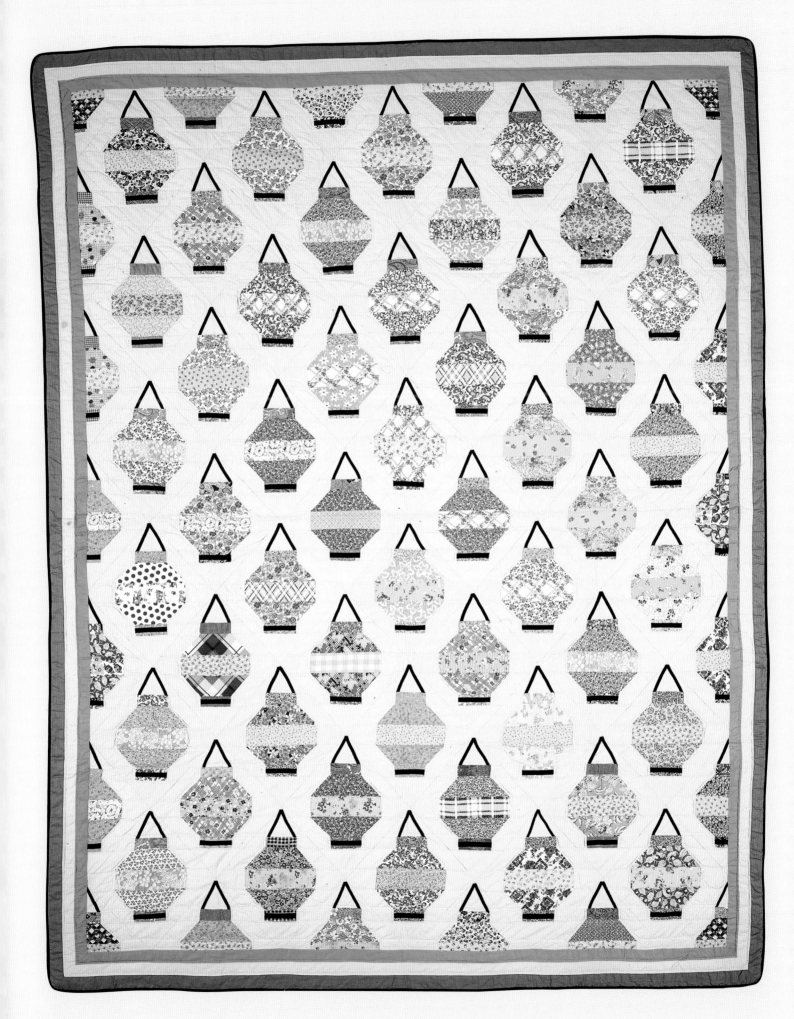

Lantern

LAURA HARMON HOWELL

1930S

USING popular pastel-colored cottons, Laura Harmon Howell pieced this lovely Lantern quilt on her farm in Broadview. Lantern designs abounded in the 1930s. Examples include patterns such as A Japanese Garden and Chinese Lantern.

Laura was born in Illinois in 1859 and married Thomas Harlan Howell in 1882. In December 1909 Laura moved from Illinois with her eight children and three grandchildren to homestead in Broadview. Thomas and their son-in-law Raymond Smith followed shortly thereafter, bringing the family's cow, horses, pigs, chickens, and Majestic stove. Her husband died in 1915, but Laura continued to run the family farm until at least 1920. She passed away in 1945, but her daughters inherited her love for quiltmaking—a Magic Vine quilt started by her daughter Minnie and finished by her daughter Edith is featured in Chapter 4.

Howell homestead, Broadview

Laura Harmon Howell

Lantern, Laura Harmon Howell, 1930s, MHQP 03-11-02 (74" x 95", cotton)

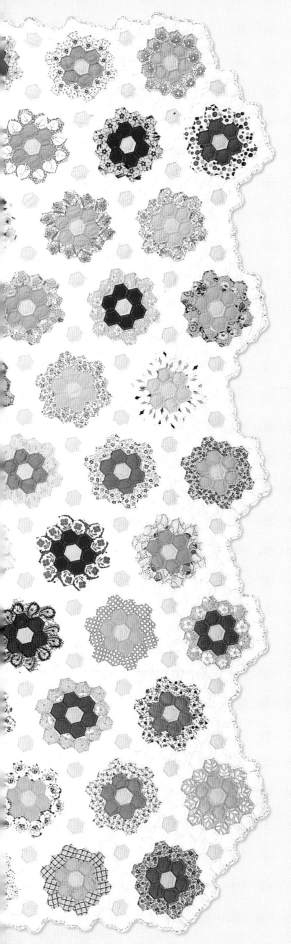

Grandmother's Flower Garden

SARA EFFIE VAN
BLARICOM WAYLETT

1933

*Sara Effie Van Blaricom
Waylett and baby*

SARA Effie Van Blaricom Waylett, who was born in Glendive in 1882 and married Bitterroot Valley farmer Herbert Waylett in 1898, pieced the top for this Grandmother's Flower Garden quilt but never finished it. Sara was well known throughout the valley as an avid quilter, and her family recalls that her neighbors would bring scraps of fabric for her to use in her quilts. She pieced everything by hand and was constantly digging through her vast reserves of material to find just the right color or pattern for her quilt.

Sara's son Fred Waylett took a particular liking to this quilt top, in part because some of the flowers contained black fabric. When Fred married Ella E. Mullis, Sara gave them the quilt top as a wedding gift. Ella tucked the top away in a cedar chest at the foot of their bed and kept it there for more than forty years. To commemorate another family marriage, Ella gave the top to her son Ray and his wife Patricia for their eleventh anniversary.

Ray and Patricia decided it was time to finish the quilt, so they entrusted the top to quilter Alma Vanacar of Victor. "Before seeing the quilt," the family recalls, "Mrs. Vanacar only promised to hand quilt part of the design, she said she would not keep the edge scalloped, and it would take as long as six months. Anxious to have the family heirloom completed, they agreed. Six weeks later, Mrs. Vanacar called to announce that the quilt was finished. . . . Mrs. Vanacar fell in love with the quilt and finished it off in all the ways she said she would not do. The quilting was done in every hexagon, the scalloped border stayed, and it only took her 6 weeks, not 6 months."[14]

*Grandmother's Flower Garden, Sara Effie
Van Blaricom Waylett, 1933, MHQP 04-92-01
(78" x 92", cotton)*

Windmill
Baby Quilt

GRACE GRAVES
MARSHALL

1938

GRACE Graves Marshall of Bozeman used a kit to make this baby quilt in 1938. Kansas-born in 1881, Grace married Earl Marshall in 1902. Between 1915 and 1920, the Marshalls moved to Bozeman, where Earl worked in a furniture store. Possibly because the baby for whom this Windmill quilt was intended turned out to be a boy and the figure is a girl, Grace's quilt was put away and never used. Her grandson Marshall Bennett inherited the quilt in 1969.

Quilt historian Sandi Fox traces the popularity of baby quilts to changing attitudes about childhood in the first half of the nineteenth century. Previously, children, particularly in the lower classes, were generally seen as small adults, and they entered the adult world of physical labor at an early age. With the rise of the middle class that accompanied industrialization, children were no longer simply treated as economic units in the household. Instead, middle-class parents put more time and resources into childrearing, and middle-class children enjoyed more time at play and in school.

As the emphasis on childhood grew, so did the importance of motherhood. The middle-class father now worked away from home, which left the mother with the primary responsibility of raising happy, moral children. As Fox explains, "By 1830, a vast number of treatises instructed [the mother] not only in the philosophical aspects of her duties but in specific and practical guidelines for every aspect of nursery life, from the child's health and dress to his education. . . . Just as society now required a woman to ensure her children's sleep, to make them safe and warm, the inclinations of her heart and hands now saw to it that they also slept in beauty."[15]

Grace Graves Marshall

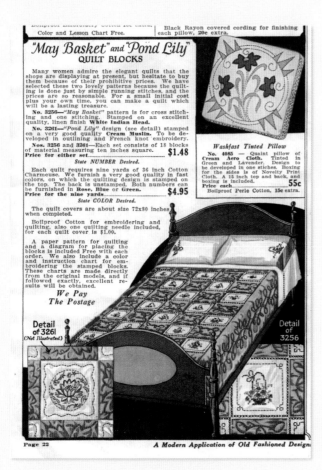

(opposite) Windmill Baby Quilt, Grace Graves Marshall, 1938, MHQP 06-157-01 (51" x 68", cotton)

(left) Mail-order catalogs made kits and patterns for embroidered quilts and other linens readily available.

Noah's Ark Baby Quilt

WILDA MAY O'NEIL
WILSON

1938

Wilda May O'Neil Wilson

THESE identical Noah's Ark baby quilts connect several generations of mothers and daughters. With the help of her mother Emma O'Neil, Wilda May Wilson made this Noah's Ark baby quilt for the birth of her daughter Barbara in 1938. Barbara recalls that the quilt rested on her bed until she was eight years old; then it was stored away. In 1988, in honor of the birth of her great-granddaughter Mallory Caitlin Pisk, Wilda May began working on an identical Noah's Ark quilt. This time Barbara helped her mother with the quilt, cutting, sketching, and keeping "the fire going and the tea water hot."[16] Mallory must have loved her great-grandmother's gift dearly, for her quilt shows more wear than its much older twin.

Aside from making lovely quilts, Wilda May was an early Kalispell pioneer and extraordinarily accomplished woman. Born to Emma and C. D. O'Neil, a lumberman, in 1907, Wilda May left Kalispell when she graduated from high school and earned an English degree at Whitman College in Walla Walla, Washington. She returned to Montana briefly to teach school in Willow Creek but left again for a year to continue her education at the American Conservatory of Music in Chicago. After Chicago, Wilda May again returned to Montana to teach fifth grade and music education in Chinook. By this time, she had embarked on a romance with Harold "Curley" Wilson, a graduate student in social welfare in Chicago, whom she had met at Whitman. The two married in 1934, living first in Chicago and then Denver, where Curley was a supervisor for the Social Security Administration.

When Curley entered the army in 1943, Wilda May moved her three young children back to Kalispell to be near her family. After the war, Wilda May and Curley purchased the general store in Olney, which they ran until Curley's sudden death in 1952. To make ends meet as a widow, Wilda May moved her family back to Kalispell and purchased a floundering hat shop downtown. She made the shop profitable by stocking yarns, embroidery floss, patterns, and notions and ran the business for nearly twenty-five years. She also put her impressive abilities to use, teaching customers new sewing skills and helping them with their projects at a round table near the window of the store.

(opposite) Noah's Ark Baby Quilt, Wilda May O'Neil Wilson, 1938, MHQP 07-281-01 (37" x 54", cotton)

(right) Noah's Ark Baby Quilt, Wilda May O'Neil Wilson, 1988, MHQP 07-282-02 (34" x 50", cotton)

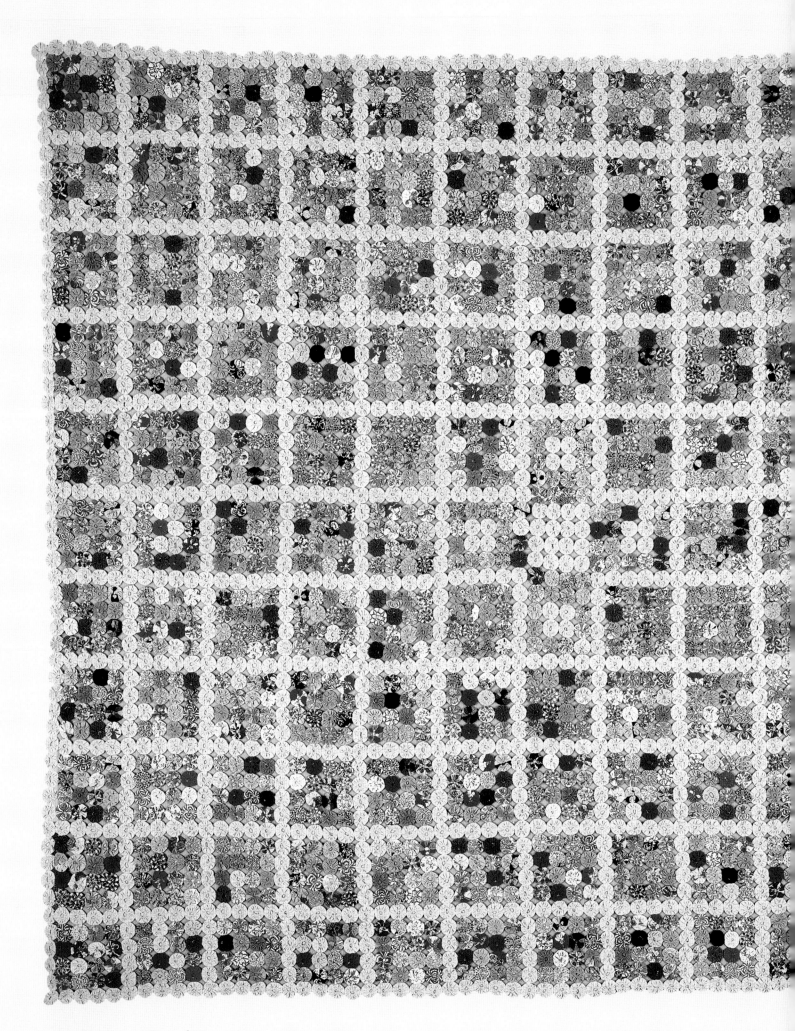

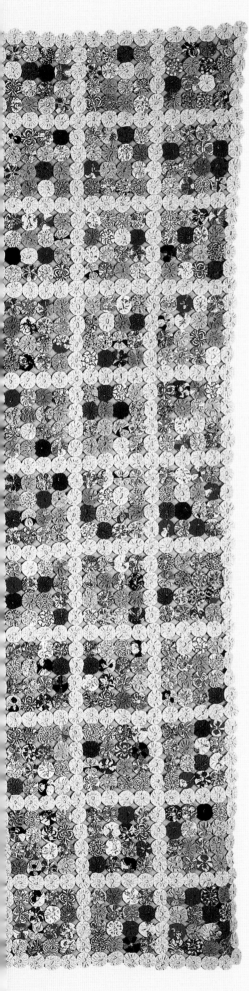

Yo-Yo

WHEN she was in the eighth grade, Edith Degner of Grass Range started making the circular "yo-yos" for this quilt but lost interest before she finished the work. Unbeknownst to Edith, her mother Tekla—who was born in Germany in 1894 and married Edward Degner in 1917—completed the process of tacking the hundreds of multicolored circles together. Edith found the finished quilt among her mother's belongings after Tekla passed away in 1977.

Like Crazy quilts, Yo-Yos are called "quilts" even though they are not generally quilted. The individual yo-yos are made by cutting circles of fabric, then putting a running stitch around the circle's edge. The fabric is gathered along the running stitch to form a pouch, and the pouch then is flattened into a circle, with the gathered edges forming the center. The tiny individual yo-yos are then joined to one another at the sides or stitched to a fabric background.

Quilt historian Virginia Gunn finds that the Yo-Yo quilt has its roots in the 1850s and 1860s, when ladies' magazines offered women tape-work patterns as cheaper, sturdier alternatives to the period's fashionable lace trims. The yo-yo technique was revived by *Peterson's Magazine* in December 1885, when columnist Helen Marion Burnside introduced a "new fancywork for ladies" that was "now but rarely seen, though once very popular."[17] In the twentieth century, the technique became popular again and was used to make everything from powder puffs to quilts such as Edith and Tekla's.

*Tekla Dengel Degner,
ca. 1915*

*Edith Degner Duty,
ca. 1975*

*Yo-Yo, Edith Degner Duty and Tekla Degner, 1938
and 1950s, MHQP 03-08-01 (88" x 102", cotton)*

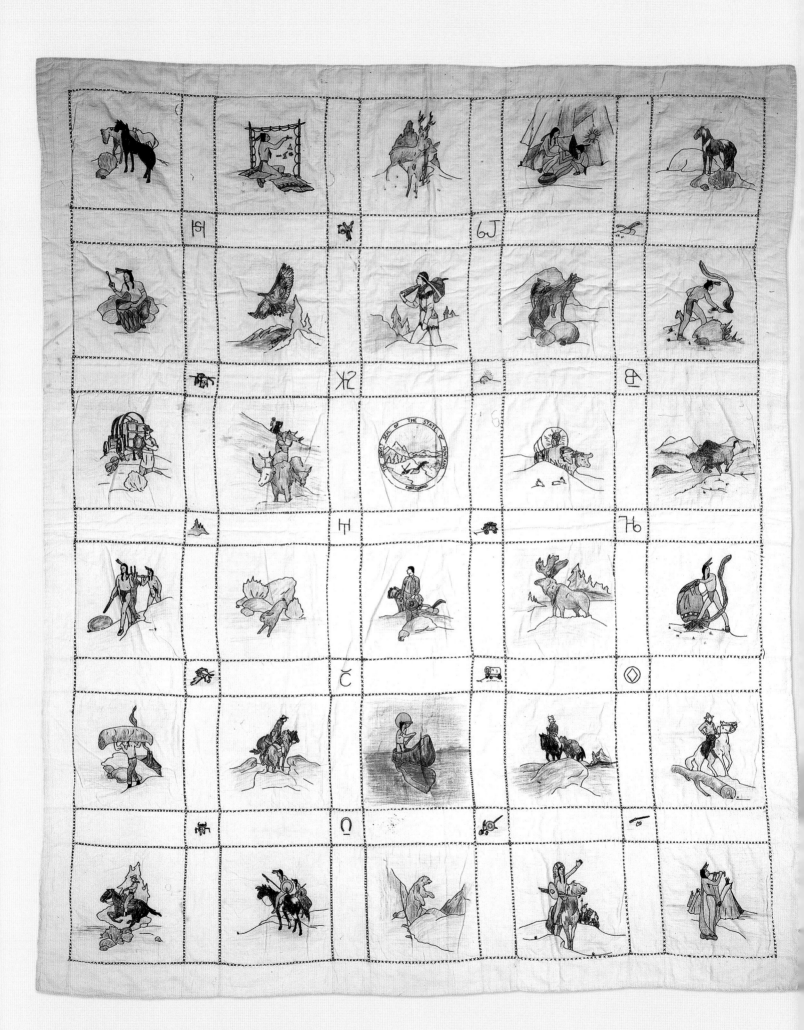

HILDA HILL SNAPP

1939

A COLORING book featuring cowboys and Indians and other western themes inspired Lewistown resident Hilda Hill Snapp's design for this quilt, which she called *Western Storybook*. Quilt historians Thomas Woodward and Blanche Greenstein hint at Hilda's possible inspiration: "'Cloth Picture Books' were suggested as a home project by *Modern Priscilla* in 1928. Unbleached muslin 'pages' were first colored with crayon, then pressed from the back with an iron to set the color, and finally outlined with stitching."[18] Hilda used this technique but collected her squares into a quilt rather than binding them together as a book. Beside the standard cowboys and Indians, Hilda added more local touches to her *Western Storybook*. She placed a block with the Montana state seal at the center and included local ranch brands on the sashing.

Born in 1911 on a ranch outside Judith Gap, Hilda Marie Hill attended college in Michigan and Billings before becoming a schoolteacher in rural Montana. She was teaching at a one-room schoolhouse in Fergus County when she met her future husband, local rancher William Snapp, at a country dance in 1936. Hilda and William married in 1938, and Hilda was pregnant with her first child when she began working on *Western Storybook*, her first quilt. Hilda's daughter-in-law Patricia Snapp recounts the quilt's story: "She 'wanted a boy so badly' but knew she should design the quilt for either a girl or a boy. Her early years of teaching in rural Montana and her love of Montana history led her to design the quilt now called 'Western Storybook.'. . . The quilt was presented to her oldest son, William J. (Bill) Snapp and me, his wife, the year after our son, also named William, was born. It was used on the bed for many years and still managed to stand up to the wear and tear with only a few broken threads. The color is faded but still there."[19]

Hilda quilted throughout her life, but it was only one of her many artistic passions. She also played the piano, wrote, painted with oils and watercolors, worked in copper, tooled leather, knitted, and crocheted. And although she quit her teaching job to work on the Snapp ranch and raise her two sons and two daughters, Hilda was a lifelong educator, teaching her many crafts through local groups such as 4-H and the Lewistown Art Center. As Pat concludes, "It's no exaggeration to say she was one of the most talented women in central Montana."[20]

Hilda Hill Snapp, ca. 2002

Western Storybook, *Hilda Hill Snapp*, 1939, MHQP 08-85-04 (71" x 84", cotton)

Dogwood Blossom

LIKE so many family quilts, this bold and intricate Dogwood Blossom quilt tells the story of one generation finishing the stitching that another generation began: Dorothy Wilson Gomon of Billings finished this quilt her grandmother had started. Gomon's granddaughter Kathie Sybrant inherited the quilt in 1978. It is not known exactly when this quilt was started, but two-color quilts such as this one were popular in the first decades of the twentieth century. *Capper's Weekly* of Topeka, Kansas, first published the Dogwood Blossom pattern in 1928. Mountain Mist also included the pattern on its batting wrappers, calling it Oklahoma Dogwood.

(above) Great-Great-Grandmother Wilson with Keith and Barbara Gomon, ca. 1937

(left) Dorothy Wilson Gomon, ca. 1970s

(far left) Dogwood Blossom, Great-Great-Grandmother Wilson, prior to 1940s, MHQP 02-51-0 (82" x 82", cotton)

CHAPTER FOUR

Modern Montana | 1940 TO 1969

World War II pulled Montana into a new era, transforming the state's economy and its culture. For the first time in decades, Montanans enjoyed economic opportunity. The war revived extractive industries by increasing the demand for lumber, metals, and coal. Farmers and ranchers received high prices for livestock and crops at the same time that unusually high rainfalls boosted yields. The need for workers in the prosperous wartime economy lured tens of thousands of Montanans to Washington, Oregon, and California for high-paying jobs in shipbuilding, aircraft manufacturing, and other lucrative defense industries.

Necktie, quiltmaker unknown, ca. 1950, MHS 1995.83.01 (detail, pieced, 43" x 57", cotton, wool, silk, rayon)

The war also brought new social and economic roles for Montana women just as it did for women nationally. Many women entered the paid workforce for the first time, some taking on jobs traditionally held by men. Juanita Putzker, a teacher in her hometown of Livingston, became an aircraft communicator for the Civil Aeronautics Administration. Juanita trained in Seattle, learning how to send and receive messages in Morse code on a teletype machine. After training, she was stationed near Whitehall, where her job was to transmit information received from pilots to the U.S. Army Air Corps in Great Falls.

Juanita describes the logistical problems encountered as women broke into the workforce: "At Whitehall, living accommodations for the staff were in the same building as the communications office, with sleeping rooms and a kitchen adjacent to the office, and a sleeping room with bunk beds in the basement. I was among three of the first women to go to that field, but since

Sew for Victory poster, 1941–1943, design by Pistchal, New York City WPA War Services

Here a female crew works on a C-47 military transport plane in the final outfitting hangar at the Great Falls Air Force Base (now Malmstrom) in June 1945.

Cowbelles' booth with the Gallatin County Cowbelles' Brand quilt at Bozeman's Montana Winter Fair, 1967. Delores Prescott is on the left; the other woman is unidentified.

there was a young man living there, we girls had to stay in a hotel in Whitehall for a time. At some point, it was decided that we could occupy the upstairs bedrooms and Chuck could be in the basement. We would share the kitchen."[1]

Montana women were also encouraged to contribute to the war effort through their domestic endeavors. Food conservation, volunteering for civil defense work, and contributing to scrap metal, rubber, paper, and grease drives all helped the war effort. The twice-monthly newspaper published jointly by the Anaconda Copper Mining Company and its unions, the *Copper Commando*, urged women to think seriously about their domestic duties, including meal planning. Serving nutritious meals in the face of the rationing of meat, butter, and sugar was no small task. "In an article plainly titled 'Thoughts for Food,'" writes historian Matt Basso, "Mrs. Smith and Mrs. Johnson talk over a common problem—what to put in the lunch bucket. 'But my John won't eat vegetables. He wants meat,' begins Mrs. Johnson. 'That's just it—' replied Mrs. Smith, 'neither will Bill and the boys. But Mrs. Griffith says we can put them in and teach them to like them. They need the energy and the right food so that the extra hours and the extra effort they're putting out won't be so hard on them.'"[2]

Fortunately, when World War II ended, Montana did not experience the kind of economic decline that had followed the previous war. Montana farmers continued to prosper through the end of the 1940s, in part because of the emerging demand for food products in California. In the 1950s and 1960s Montana agriculture returned to its familiar boom-and-bust cycle, experienc-

ing some good years and some bad. Montana's farmers and ranchers, however, were better able to weather these cycles with the help of federal aid, increased mechanization, and more scientific management.

As the demand for copper waned in the years immediately following the war, the Anaconda Company turned to new methods of extraction to keep its Montana operations afloat. In the mid-1950s the company began the practice of extracting ore from an open pit rather than an underground tunnel. Open-pit mining was a double-edged sword for Butte. It ensured, at least temporarily, the continued economic presence

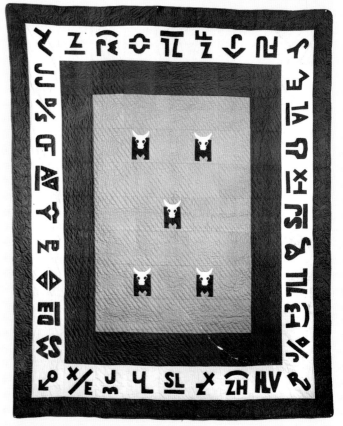

Big Horn Cowbelles' Brand quilt (appliquéd), 1961

State Flowers and Birds, Edith Howell Frey and Marjorie Arneson, after 1959, MHQP 03-11-03 (87" x 100", blends)

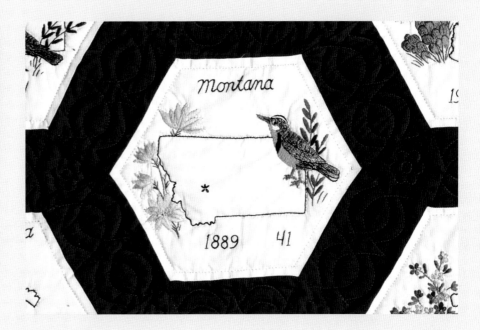

Marjorie Arneson, left, and her mother Edith Howell Frey put a few stitches into the Montana Centennial quilt.

of the Anaconda Company. But the Berkeley Pit, which opened in 1955, eventually swallowed enormous portions of the historic uptown. More troubling for Butte's workers was the gradual loss of jobs: open-pit mining was more automated than underground mining.

After the war, other extractive industries surpassed the copper industry in importance to Montana's economy. In the prosperous 1950s, Montana's forests served the nationwide demand for lumber. Wood products industries—including paper, plywood, and formaldehyde companies—followed in the 1960s. Oil production, which began in the 1920s in Montana, also increased after the war, particularly with the 1951 discovery of major oil fields in the Williston Basin. Some Montana oil fields yielded natural gas as well, and Montana produced over twenty billion cubic feet of natural gas every year throughout the 1950s.

Change could be noted on all fronts during the three decades that stretched from the beginning of World War II through the 1960s, including in the area of women's handwork. Generally, quilt historians point to the beginning of that war as the end of the early-twentieth-century quilt revival. It's no surprise that women abandoned quiltmaking during the war given the demands on their time and the fabric rationing that made cloth other than feed sacks difficult to find.

In the postwar years the continued decline in quiltmaking can be traced to changing aesthetics. Middle-class Americans were eager to settle down, start families, and build new houses, and they embraced modernism because it suggested progress—a break from the past in favor of a bright, optimistic future. Fashionable women put their antique furniture in the garage and their quilts in cedar chests, instead decorating their living rooms with Danish modern furniture and draping their beds with easy-to-wash synthetic blankets. Quilts looked stuffy and old-fashioned in clean-lined, simple modernist interiors.

Of course, some Montana women continued the art of quiltmaking. The December 15, 1968, *Billings Gazette* featured a story about one such Montana quilter, Hazel McCracken, who grew up on a ranch west of Billings and homesteaded with her husband in the Pryor Mountains before moving to Billings in 1917. Hazel's mother taught her to quilt when she was eleven, and she continued making quilts well into old age. The *Gazette* reporter noted that "[i]nside her white cottage beneath the towering cottonwoods are piles of quilts, afghans, numerous plants and collections of china cups and saucers, plates and figurines. . . . Just this past year she has made 19 baby quilts and 12 full-size ones." Hazel's quilts won several ribbons at Billings's Midland Empire State Fair: "The first quilt she made as a child won first prize as the oldest at the 1966 fair. A blue ribbon winner of 1964 is a bright silk puff quilt 'It takes a year to make one like that,' she says. 'the quilt has [over 900] puffs, each filled with old nylon stockings.'"[3]

The women from Montana's rural areas whose quilts appear in this chapter—women like Edith Howell Frey, with her 1940s Magic Vine quilt, and Mary Kent Stevens, with her 1950s Bull Durham quilt—kept their mothers' art of quiltmaking alive. Their skills would again be appreciated when the twentieth century's second "quilt revival" took hold in the 1970s. ❖

THIS Magic Vine quilt linked two sisters who inherited their love of quilting from their mother, the prodigious quiltmaker Laura Harmon Howell, whose Lantern quilt is featured in Chapter 3. Sisters Minnie Mabel Howell Smith and Edith Howell moved with their large extended family from Illinois to Broadview, northwest of Billings, in 1909. Minnie, born in 1882, was already married to Raymond Smith and had a son, but her youngest sister Edith was only nine when their parents Laura and Thomas Howell made a new start homesteading in Montana.

When Minnie found quilt patterns she liked in newspapers, she immediately purchased the fabric and then stored the fabrics and patterns together in packets to be made into quilts at a later date. Minnie did not get around to using the fabric she collected for this Magic Vine quilt, but Edith, who married Conrad Frey of Broadview in 1924, found her sister's packet and decided to make the quilt. Edith gave this quilt to Minnie's oldest daughter Nina, but she liked the pattern so much that she made two others just like it for each of her own children.

Magic Vine

EDITH HOWELL FREY
1940s

Edith Howell Frey, center, with her sisters Mayme and Maude

Magic Vine, Edith Howell Frey, 1940s, MHQP 03-14-01 (87" x 106", blends)

Dresden Plate, Katherine Liddle McEvoy, 1941, MHQP 22-68-01 (69" x 84", cotton)

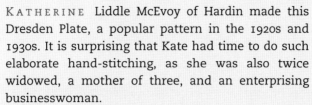

Dresden Plate

KATHERINE LIDDLE
McEVOY

1941

KATHERINE Liddle McEvoy of Hardin made this Dresden Plate, a popular pattern in the 1920s and 1930s. It is surprising that Kate had time to do such elaborate hand-stitching, as she was also twice widowed, a mother of three, and an enterprising businesswoman.

Born in Wisconsin in 1864, Kate married Ed Bowler in 1882, and the couple had three children. In 1890 the Bowler family moved to Butte, and after Ed died in 1897, Kate married J. C. McEvoy. Widowed again in 1903, two years later she moved her three children to Billings, where she ran a restaurant.

In the spring of 1908 Kate relocated to Hardin, a small town on the edge of the Crow Reservation. She started out managing the dining room of the Hardin Hotel, the town's only hotel and dining room. A few months later Kate purchased a lot on West Center Avenue, built a boardinghouse, and opened for business. She advertised in the January 1909 *Hardin Tribune*: "McEvoy House, elegantly furnished rooms. Board and room by the day or week, and meals like Mother cooked."[4]

Facing new competition from the McEvoy House, the Hardin Hotel's owner, Mattie Anderson, decided to close and remodel her dining room. When she reopened three months later, however, she no longer had her restaurant manager and offered the space to Kate. Kate decided to lease the dining room, which meant that she controlled two-thirds of the restaurant trade in Hardin. In 1912 Kate purchased the Hardin Hotel, and she owned it until shortly before her death in 1942.

Katherine Liddle McEvoy's Hardin Hotel

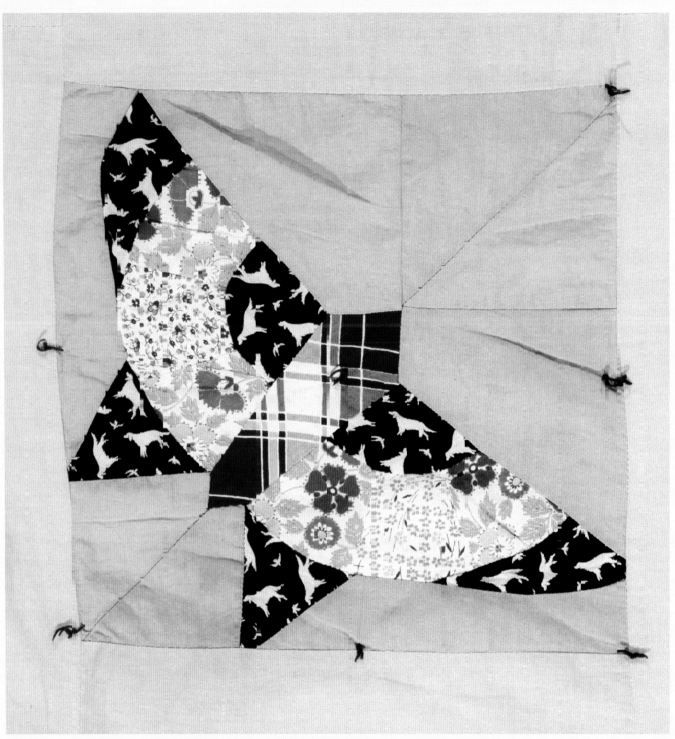

Butterfly, Margaret Adelia Rounds Jensen, ca. 1940, MHQP 02-66-01 *(73" x 85", cotton)*

Butterfly

MARGARET ADELIA
ROUNDS JENSEN

ca. 1940

USING a pattern published by the Old Chelsea Station Needlecraft Company around 1935, Margaret Adelia Rounds Jensen pieced this Butterfly quilt with her daughter Leila Williams. Leila inherited the quilt when her mother died.

In 1966 Leila also helped her mother publish her memoir, *Looking Back,* which offers a glimpse into the life of a farm wife during Montana's homesteading era. Margaret was born in Texas and married her husband John Jensen in Tulsa, Oklahoma, in 1912. Shortly after they wed, the Jensens moved to Nebraska, where John worked as a carpenter. Margaret, who had grown up on a farm and vowed never to marry a farmer "because they were always moving and had to work so hard all the time," found herself discontented with life as a carpenter's wife. "I didn't like sitting around the house all day doing nothing," she recalled. "Everything we ate came out of the grocery store, and everything was so quiet. It was such a different way of life than I had known and I wished I was back on the farm so I could do something."[5]

In the summer of 1914, Margaret got her wish. The Jensens and their two young children moved to Montana to homestead. After a temporary stay in Billings, they started a farm seven miles southwest of Columbus in Stillwater County. The family raised wheat and during the Depression purchased neighboring farms as people left the area. In 1938 they were prosperous enough to purchase a combine. Margaret remembered the machine fondly because, in addition to decreasing the work at harvest, it "saved a lot of kitchen work, too, as we didn't have to cook for all those men at threshing time. What a relief that was!"[6] John and Margaret continued to run the farm until 1947, when their sons returned from serving in World War II and took over. The couple then retired and moved to Columbus.

Margaret Jensen and her husband John

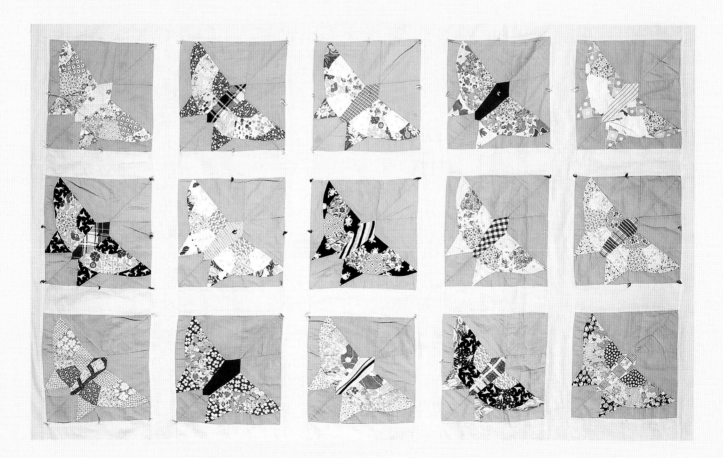

LADIES
COUNCIL
E Magnuson

PSALMS
31:24

BAPTIST
COMMUNITY
CHURCH
Mrs Bentley

1 COR.
2:9

CROW AGENCY
MONTANA

Ida Egolf

Mrs. C. Larson

Mrs Dell   Louk

Mrs Wagner

Edna Davis

Ginny Newman

Mrs Magnuson

Mrs Borland

Mrs W. Gentry

E. M. Boggess

E. Scalig.

J. L. Ford

Mrs S. P. Louk

Mrs W. L.   Halap

A. Peck

Susie Denny

Mrs Roberts

Amy E. Hyde

Mrs Warren

Mrs G. L.   Lyle

Friendship Dahlia

LADIES COUNCIL OF THE
CROW AGENCY BAPTIST
COMMUNITY CHURCH

1940

THE Ladies Council of the Crow Agency Baptist Community Church presented Ruth Turner Knight with this lovely Friendship Dahlia quilt as a going-away gift when she moved from Hardin to Billings in 1940. Ruth was born in Minnesota in 1875 and taught school in Webster, South Dakota, after she attended junior college. She married Daniel Knight in Webster in 1896, and the couple moved to the Sarpy area. When Ruth was widowed in 1930, she moved to Crow Agency, and then to nearby Hardin in 1933. Her friendship quilt bears the signatures of more than thirty members of the local community, including Laura Paine Bentley, a Baptist minister and wife of church pastor Chester Bentley.

The Bentleys moved to the Crow Reservation in 1923 after they received an appointment from the Baptist Home Mission Society to serve as missionaries among the local Indians. Laura's obituary observes, "She was very active in working with the children and women's programs of the church. She enjoyed her associations with the Indian women at the weekly sewing meetings."[7]

Even after she moved to Billings, Ruth remained close to Laura. Shortly before her death in 1971, Ruth gave this quilt to Laura, who in turn donated it to the Big Horn County Historical Society.

Quilt recipient Ruth Turner Knight

Friendship Dahlia, Ladies Council of the Crow Agency Baptist Community Church, 1940, MHQP 22-00-36 (75" x 85", cotton)

Yo-Yo

ANNA MARY GRIFFITH

ca. 1940

ANNA Mary Griffith made this brightly colored, zigzagging Yo-Yo quilt as a wedding gift for her granddaughter Irene Evers of Missoula.

Born in 1915, Irene was an extraordinary woman and holds a small but special place in the history of Missoula. She started working as the librarian for the University of Montana's forestry school in 1959 and did not retire until 1997. She was by then in her early eighties. In 1976, when the forestry collection moved to the Maureen and Mike Mansfield Library, Irene moved with it and became the assistant science librarian. The university honored her dedication twice: in 1993 the library created the Irene Evers Award for Outstanding Staff, and in 1995, in honor of her eightieth birthday, the forestry school's faculty, staff, and former students pooled their money to create the Irene Evers Endowment for Forestry.

The full scope of Irene's commitment to her work, however, was not fully realized until after her death in 1999. Irene lived a simple, frugal life, and many of her co-workers assumed that financial hardship forced her to work well past the age of retirement. They were stunned to find out after her death that Irene had willed her entire estate of $650,000 to the Mansfield Library and the School of Forestry. The money was used to support scholarships for forestry students and to further build the Evers Endowment for Forestry.

Irene must have also recognized the value of preserving Montana's historic textiles. She donated her treasured wedding quilt to the Historical Museum at Fort Missoula.

Irene Evers, right, and Anna Mary Griffith, second from left, and three unidentified women, ca. 1945

Yo-Yo, Anna Mary Griffith,
ca. 1940, MHQP 04-12-08
(64" x 82", cotton)

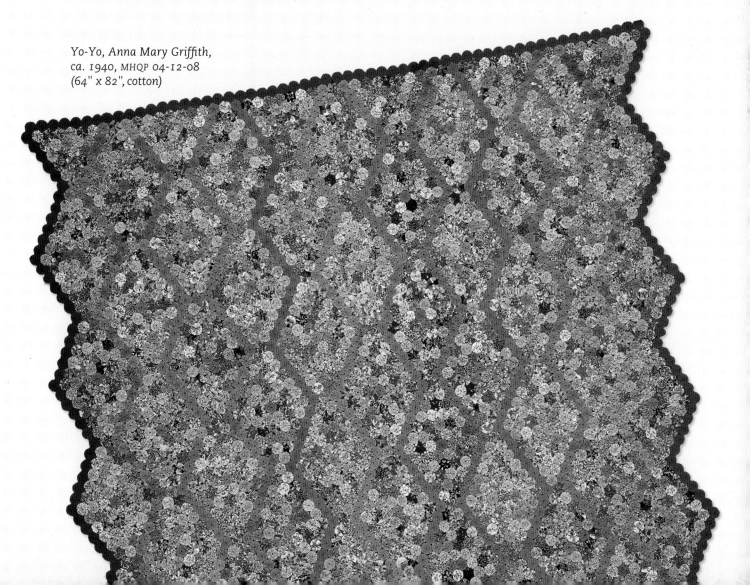

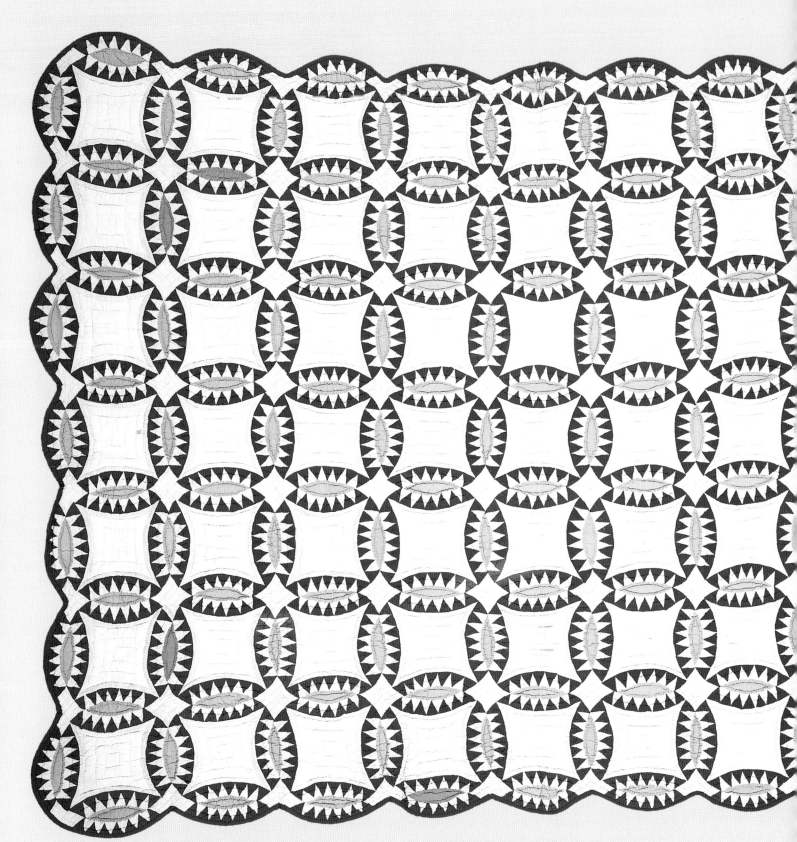

Indian Wedding Ring, Sarah Walker Pease, 1940s, MHQP 22-146-01 (60" x 78", cotton)

Indian Wedding Ring

SARAH WALKER PEASE

1940S

THIS bold and complex Indian Wedding Ring (or Pickle Dish) is a testament to the spirit of Sarah Walker Pease, a Hidatsa–Scotch Irish ranch wife and shopkeeper who survived the deaths of her parents, a child, and a husband. Throughout her life, she created beautiful handcrafts.

Born in North Dakota in 1866, Sarah spent her early childhood on the Fort Berthold Reservation. At the age of thirteen, she was sent to the Hampton Institute, an Indian boarding school in Virginia. Her parents died while she was there.

In 1885 Sarah accepted a position at Bonds Unitarian Christian Industrial School for Crow Indians in the lower Bighorn Valley. There she met George Pease, a Crow Indian employed at the Catholic Indian Mission at St. Xavier. The two married in 1888 and started a ranch on their allotted land on Rotten Grass Creek in the foothills of the Bighorn Mountains. In 1905 the Peases' children were removed to the Crow Agency Boarding School. Shortly after arriving at the school, their five-year-old son Oliver became seriously ill. The Peases were notified that Oliver was sick, but they were unable to complete the fifty-mile wagon trip to the school before he died.

The Peases sold their ranch to the Heinrich Cattle Company in 1907 and moved to Lodge Grass, where George opened the Indian Trading Store in 1909. George had his leg amputated and died from the resulting blood loss in 1916, leaving Sarah a widow at age fifty. In her memoir *Reaching Both Ways*, Sarah's daughter Helen Pease Wolf remembered how her mother kept the family together even as four of her sons were drafted into the army in World War I.

Helen also remembers her mother's exquisite handcrafts: "Sarah, after raising her family, now took time to put into motion her natural ability of Indian lore. Her creative ability came forth in her designing of bead belts, bags, and moccasins. She made Indian dolls and dressed them in native costumes that were true to life. She also created wall hangings in minute color and design depicting scenes of early Indian village life."[8] At the end of her life, Sarah also hand-stitched quilts for each of her children. This Indian Wedding Ring was one of them.

(*above*) *Sarah Walker Pease, ca. 1908*
(*below*) *Sarah's daughter Helen Pease Wolf with one of her mother's last Wedding Ring quilts, ca. 1985*

Bull Durham Patchwork, Mary Kent Stevens, 1950s, MHQP 22-64-01 *(66" x 76", cotton)*

Bull Durham Patchwork

MARY KENT STEVENS

1950S

THIS lovely quilt is an example of the resourcefulness of a quilter who created something beautiful with the simple materials she had on hand. Mary Kent Stevens, a Crow woman from Lodge Grass, used Bull Durham tobacco bags to create vivid patchwork quilts for each of her grandsons. This quilt, with alternating dyed green patches, was given to Mick Stevens of Lodge Grass in the 1950s.

Rural American women frequently recycled feed and flour sacks to make quilts in the nineteenth and early twentieth centuries. Because the large amount of fabric needed to make a bed-sized quilt could be prohibitively expensive, sacks became a good source of material for eager quilters.

As quilt historian Marsha MacDowell explains, sacks have long been a choice source of material among Native American quilters. She cites a commentary by Georgia Rae Easter, a home extension agent on the Pine Ridge Reservation in the 1930s, on the particular popularity of tobacco bags. Easter wrote in 1935: "Men 'roll' their own in the Sioux country, cowboy fashion, a custom which causes local traders to stock large quantities of sacked tobacco upon their shelves. Mary [Scout] saves every tobacco bag which her husband, Jasper, empties and hides away until she has a quantity sufficient to start work. The yellow draw strings are then carefully untied, pulled out, and laid in strands. The bags are turned wrong side out and the thread raveled from the lockstitched seams. Not one inch of thread is wasted, for practice enables Mary to rip a seam without breaking a thread. Next comes preparation for wash day. Mary carries the water from the Creek, seventy-five paces from below the house, and allows it to stand overnight until all silt settles to the bottom. The water is heated with wood which she cuts herself—for the Indian country women often cut the wood. With homemade soap she washes the yellow draw strings, the thread taken from the ripped seams, and the muslin. When nicely ironed, the origin of the lovely white pieces of muslin could never be guessed."[9]

Mary Kent Stevens

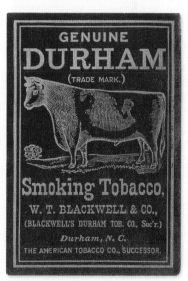

Durham Smoking Tobacco label

Cross-Stitch Floral Wreath

BEULAH L. Gaither, who worked as a registered nurse in East St. Louis before moving to Drakesboro, Kentucky, began this cross-stitch Floral Wreath quilt in 1957 as a bridal quilt for her granddaughter Mary Wallace, even though Mary was only one year old at the time. One year later, when Beulah was diagnosed with cancer, her friends pitched in to finish Mary's quilt: two friends finished the cross-stitching, and the women of the Ladies Aid Society of the First Methodist Church in Collinsville, Illinois, which Beulah had presided over for twenty years, did the quilting. Beulah did not have the chance to see her granddaughter marry, as she passed away in October 1959. But when Mary announced her engagement in 1976, she was presented with this lovely keepsake from her grandmother.

Cross-stitch quilt kits became popular in the 1950s. The prestamped x's made cross-stitch quilts easy enough to make as long as the quiltmaker had the patience required to make thousands of tiny stitches.

BEULAH L. POWELL GAITHER

1957

Nurse and quiltmaker Beulah L. Powell Gaither with her daughter Suzanne and granddaughter Mary Wallace, ca. 1956

Cross-stitch Floral Wreath, Beulah L. Powell Gaither, 1957, MHQP 07-318-01 *(76" x 88", cotton)*

Windblown Tulips, Kula Moss Arnold, 1958, MHQP 03-15-01, Moss Mansion 88.13.18 (72" x 80", cotton)

KULA MOSS ARNOLD
1958

KULA Moss Arnold, the daughter of prominent Billings banker and community leader Preston Boyd Moss and his wife Martha Ursula Woodson Moss, hand-pieced this Windblown Tulips quilt in 1958. Her maid Maggie Vander Voorden helped Kula with the hand-quilting.

Born in Paris, Missouri, in 1891, Kula came to Montana with her parents and older brother Woodson Jackson in 1892. Kula and her younger sister Melville homesteaded in the Garvin Basin until she married John Bingle Arnold, a Billings banker, in 1923. The couple had one son, John Jr., who died at the young age of seven. John Sr. passed away in 1948, and Kula died of a heart attack ten years later, the same year that she and Maggie made this quilt. Several of Kula's quilts, including her Windblown Tulips, are now on display at the Moss Mansion Historic House Museum in Billings.

A well-known pattern, Windblown Tulips was designed by quilt entrepreneur Marie D. Webster and published in her 1915 book, *Quilts: Their Story and How to Make Them*. The pattern uses two Dutch motifs—tulips and spinning windmills—to create the image of flowers being blown by a strong wind. A renowned quilt designer who was strongly influenced by the colonial revival, Webster got her start in 1911 when *Ladies' Home Journal* published several of her patterns. These patterns sparked a renewed interest in appliqué and influenced the floral patterns and pastel colors that typified quilts of the 1920s and 1930s. Webster transformed her overnight celebrity into a thriving business, the Practical Patchwork Company, which marketed quilt kits and finished quilts made from Webster's patterns. The success of her book launched Webster into a successful lecturing career. According to *A Joy Forever: Marie Webster's Quilt Patterns,* a biography written by her granddaughter Rosalind Webster Perry, Webster adhered meticulously to her colonial-revival aesthetic—she even showed up for her talks dressed in early American costume.

Kula Moss Arnold, 1923

Windblown Tulips on a bed in the Moss Mansion, 2008

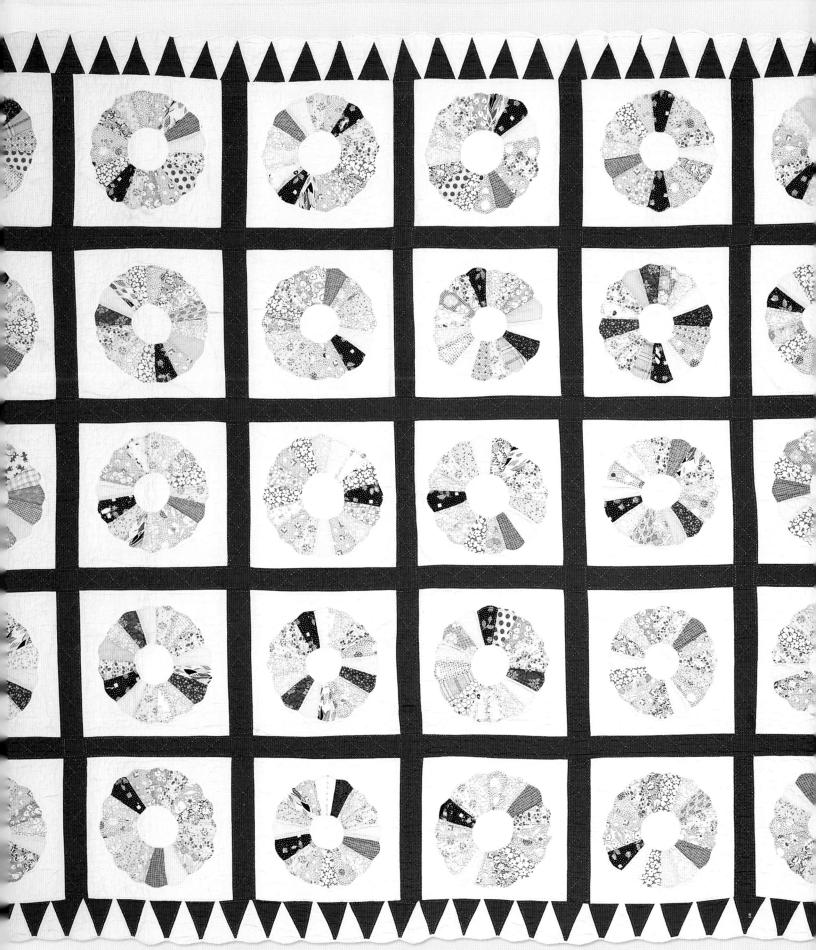

Dresden Plate, Hilda Dyrdahl and Mary Behrman, 1958–1959, MHQP 05-78-01 *(69" x 81", cotton, rayon)*

Dresden Plate

HILDA DYRDAHL &
MARY BEHRMAN

1958–1959

THIS dark, rich Dresden Plate quilt was started by Phillips County homesteader Hilda Dyrdahl and then, as her health began to fail, was completed by her friend and former neighbor Mary Behrman. Born in Minnesota to Norwegian immigrants, Hilda Dyrdahl and her husband George came to northern Phillips County to homestead in 1910. She began to sew this quilt in the 1940s and worked on the blocks for several years, but in 1958 Hilda's friend Mary Berhman took up the task of finishing the quilt. Mary and her husband H. H. had also farmed in Phillips County in the 1910s, and they remained close to the Dyrdahls because their daughter married Hilda and George's son.

Mary finished this lovely quilt in Kalispell in 1959, shortly before Hilda passed away in Owatonna, Minnesota. The quilt is especially precious to its current owner, Cathryn Dyrdahl York, because it was made by both her maternal and paternal grandmothers.

Hilda Dyrdahl and her granddaughter Cathryn, age three

Mary Behrman and her husband H. H. in front of their sod house

Tulips, Hazel Bainter Wilder, late 1960s, MHQP 19-36-04 (82" x 88", cotton)

Tulips

HAZEL BAINTER WILDER
late 1960s

HAZEL Bainter Wilder made this bright, unique Tulip quilt sometime in the late 1960s and brought it to Montana on a visit to her daughter Phyllis Wilder Jewell. Phyllis believes that the design is original because her mother experimented with the same tulip pattern in six other quilts. Hazel's quilt is unique for its on-point block arrangement as well as for the choice of vibrant and varied cotton prints in the center petals of the quilt's flowers—no two tulips are alike.

Born in 1900 in LaHarpe, Illinois, Hazel moved with her family to Missouri when she was twelve. During World War I, she and her sister Helena taught in rural Missouri schools. Hazel married her husband Philip after the war, and the couple farmed first in Missouri and then in Colorado. Hazel continued to teach until the couple's daughter was born in 1923.

Their farm struggled in the drought years of the Great Depression, so in 1936 the Wilders moved to Grand Junction, Colorado, to look for work. There, Hazel held various jobs, including ones at a seed company, peach-packing shed, and tea room, besides fulfilling her everyday duties as a mother, wife, and homemaker. In 1972 the Wilders moved to Fort Benton, Montana, to be near Phyllis, their only daughter, and her family.

Hazel Bainter Wilder, 1969

CHAPTER FIVE

Quilting Revival | 1970 TO THE PRESENT

Over the past forty years, Montanans have been enthusiastic quilters. Surely one of the reasons they quilt with such passion today is that quilting anchors them to a place and to the women in their past. For these quilters, quiltmaking is outside fashion: it is a craft that they love and a way to maintain a part of their heritage.

Centennial quilt, Audrey Levitan, 1989, MHS 1989.19.01. This quilt won the Curator's Choice Award when displayed in the Montana State Centennial Commemorative Quilt Exhibit in 1989 and was subsequently acquired for the Montana Historical Society Museum collection. Made of cotton cloth, the quilt measures 61" x 81".

Puerto Rican Christmas Parade,
*Suzanne Huston, 2001, MHQP 12-07-03
(35" x 43", cotton)*

In its current enthusiasm for quilting, Montana has taken part in a national quilting revival similar to the one that swept the country in the 1920s and 1930s. Quilt historians attribute the most recent interest in quilts to the convergence of two social and political developments of the 1960s and 1970s: the counterculture movement and feminism. The so-called "hippies" are now most famous for their protests of the Vietnam War and experimentation with illicit substances, but proponents of the counterculture movement were also searching for an alternative to what seemed to be an increasingly corporate, artificial, impersonal world. In the search for a simpler lifestyle, they developed a new respect for traditional handcrafts. Skills like knitting, crocheting, woodworking, and, of course, quiltmaking presented personal and local alternatives to mass production and consumerism.

Feminism also renewed respect for women's work. Although some feminists rejected traditional handcrafts, others deeply valued women's needlework because it represented the important contributions that women's domestic work had made to American history. Quilting, perhaps more than any other traditional craft, has come to symbolize women's meaningful domestic roles. We associate quilts with maternal warmth—both physical and metaphorical. We see in quilts the everyday beauty that women brought to their families. Above all, quilts represent hard work and meticulous craftsmanship. They tell the overlooked tales of women's lives.

As new ideas about the meaning of quilts began to gain currency, artists, collectors, and curators started to view quilts as works of art. One of the turning points occurred in 1971 when the Whitney Museum of American Art in New York held an exhibition titled "Abstract Design in American Quilts." Inspired, myriad artists, many of whom received training in disciplines such as drawing, painting, and sculpture, chose to pick up a needle. The resulting phenomenon is the art quilt, a quilt that uses fabric as a medium of artistic expression and is generally meant to be hung on a wall rather than draped on a bed.

As textiles have offered new ways to experiment with color, texture, and pattern, art quilts have become as popular in Montana as elsewhere. Suzanne Huston of Havre is one of many Montana artists to take up quilting. She focused on painting for many years, but lately quilts have become her canvas. Suzanne designed the blocks for the Hi-Line Quilt Guild's *Petticoats and Prairies* featured at the end of this chapter. Her own *Puerto Rican Christmas Parade* (above) was inspired by a photograph from a family vacation.

Other Montana quilters have been experimenting with new technologies to give traditional designs a modern twist. The photo-transfer quilt pictured on the facing page melds photography with a more traditional block-and-sash style to create a modern family album. Made by Pam Lambott and Linda Kitto of Toston and Barb Durkee of Helena, *Shadow Box of Memories* commemorates the fiftieth wedding anniversary of Toston couple Marion and Forrest Kitto in 1999. Through photographs, the blocks capture the family, their hobbies, and the important events that shaped the Kittos' five-decade marriage. The quilt is now very precious to the family, as Forrest passed away less than a month after the celebration. Because early photo-transfer technology was not yet perfected, the photographs turned brittle and began to crack and peel after only a few years, and the family is taking special care to preserve the blocks on this quilt.

Shadow Box of Memories, *Pam Lambott, Linda Kitto, and Barb Durkee, 1999,* MHQP 43-03-01 *(58" x 79", cotton)*

Bozeman Centennial, *Susan Davis, 1983,* MHQP 06-148-07
(40" x 60", *cotton*)

Susan Davis with her Bozeman
Centennial *quilt*

Montana itself often serves as a muse for contemporary quilters, and the state's rich past and its striking and varied landscape appear over and over again in contemporary quilts. For instance, Susan Davis made the appliqué quilt above to commemorate the hundredth anniversary of the incorporation of Bozeman. Along with the mountains, flowers, and wheat fields for which the Gallatin Valley is famous, Susan's quilt depicts such Bozeman landmarks as Montana State University, the historic Bozeman Opera House, and the old Langhor Ranger Station.

Other Montana quiltmakers choose to honor the state's rich Indian history. Take John Flynn's *Crazy Horse,* which is not a quilt but a piece of public art that features a "skin" made using the methods of Crazy quilting. *Crazy Horse* was one of thirty-five fiberglass horse sculptures decorated to raise money for the restoration of the historic Billings train depot. John, a professional quilter and quilt-frame designer, asked quilter and history teacher Mary Beth Billstein to help him

come up with the names of historic figures to be embroidered on the "quilt." Quilter Jerry Belgarde handbeaded the horse's eyes and encouraged John to add the names of prominent Indian quilters Almira Jackson and Bridget Fast Horse. The convergence of art, quilting, and Montana's native past was a hit: *Crazy Horse* garnered a bid of twelve thousand dollars from Johnnie Thomas of Miles City. It now resides in the Miles City Community College Library.

John Flynn is just one of the many talented quilters working in Montana today. We can feature only a few of them, but the amazing work of Montana's contemporary quiltmakers could fill volumes. Treasured by their families and enjoyed by members of their communities today, their quilts will soon enough be important artifacts that tell of Montana's history. ❖

Crazy Horse, *John Flynn and others, 2002*

John Flynn and Crazy Horse, 2002

BORN south of Rosebud in 1908, Doris Cass married Robert Miller in 1938 and was a homemaker in Big Timber when she hand-embroidered and hand-quilted this State Birds and Flowers quilt in 1970. The *Omaha World Herald* first published the pattern for this quilt throughout the months of 1938. The pattern featured forty-eight blocks representing the states that comprised the United States that year.

Made after Alaska and Hawaii became states, Doris's quilt features fifty embroidered blocks. It also displays a humorous Montana twist. Deciding there were enough meadowlarks on the quilt, Doris replaced Montana's state bird with a hand-drawn magpie, a bird much maligned by ranchers because of its aggressive behavior and tendency to harass livestock. Three years after finishing the quilt, Doris gave it to her daughter Myrna Mack Aamold, who lives in Hobson.

Doris Cass Miller, right, with her husband Robert and daughter Myrna

State Birds and Flowers, Doris Cass Miller, 1970, MHQP 36-39-02 (68" x 83", cotton, blends)

Postage Stamp around the World, Mabel Conard Lucas, 1974, MHQP 08-86-10 (81" x 89", cotton)

Postage Stamp around the World

MABEL CONARD LUCAS

1974

Mabel Conard Lucas

MABEL Conard Lucas crafted this vibrant Postage Stamp around the World quilt in 1974. The quilt is remarkably square and uniform, especially considering that Mabel pieced it completely by hand from individual squares, starting with the center squares and meticulously working her way out to the edges.

Mabel's love of quiltmaking began at a young age. When she was seven, she pieced the blocks for the Puss in the Corner quilt pictured below. At the time, Mabel's father Theodore Conard was the foreman on a farm owned by Theodore Hogeland on Warm Spring Creek in Fergus County. Hogeland's wife Emma helped Mabel put together the quilt, sparking in the child a lifelong passion for quilting. In 1947 Mabel married Andrew Lucas, a local rancher, and she continued to quilt throughout her life, on her own and with the Women's Club in Danvers.

Quiltmaking, it would seem, was just one of Mabel's talents. The August 11, 1949, *Billings Gazette* listed her as a first-place winner in the Midland Empire Fair 4-H contest for her Desoto plums.

Puss in the Corner,
Mabel Conard and Emma Hogeland,
ca. 1919, MHQP 08-86-09
(78" x 78", cotton)

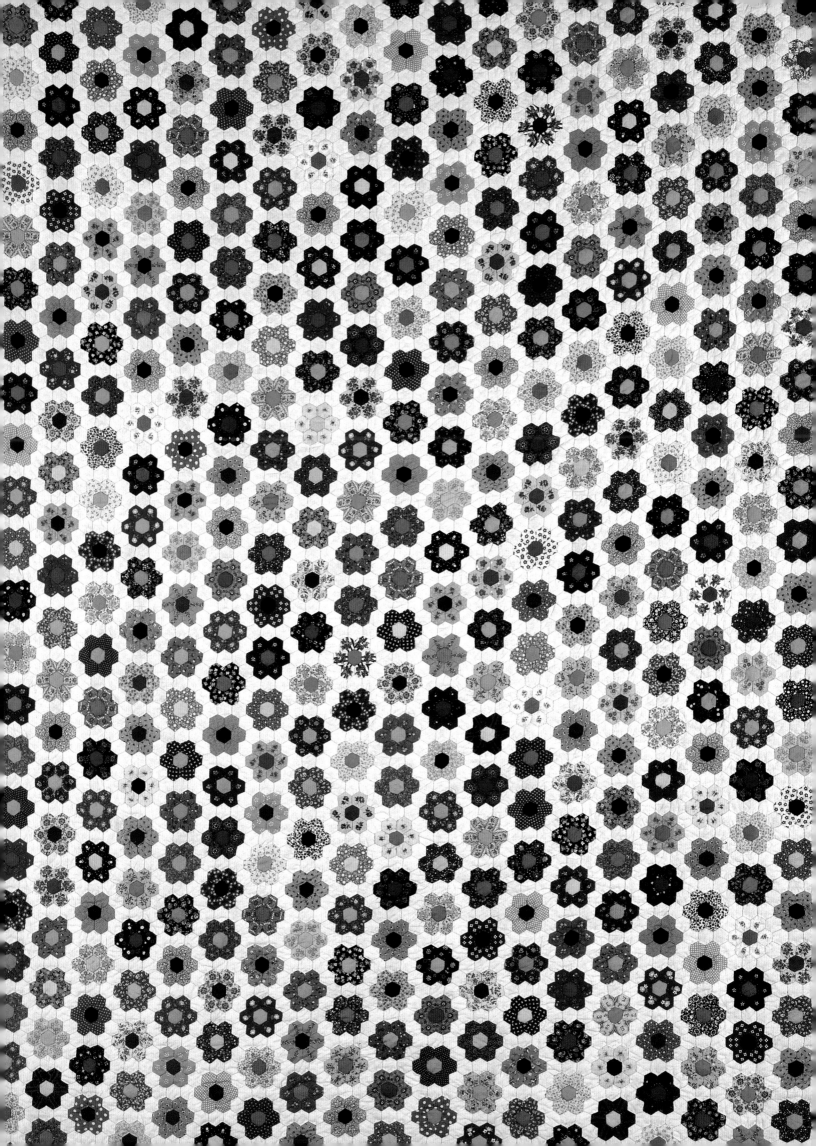

Grandmother's Flower Garden

MARY HORNSETH

1980

MARY Hornseth of Salem, Oregon, spent more than a year meticulously hand-piecing the squares of this postage stamp–sized Grandmother's Flower Garden quilt. Her daughter Elaine Graber of Kalispell remembers Mary working on her quilt while the rest of her family boated and water-skied on Lake Blaine. Mary saved up thousands of tiny pieces of fabric over the years, including some from Elaine's high school dresses. In 1988 Mary gave the quilt to Elaine and her husband as a twenty-fifth anniversary gift.

Born in Canada to Austro-Hungarian immigrants, Mary learned to sew when she went to work at a garment factory at the age of fourteen. She married an American and became a citizen in 1946. Although she designed and sewed Elaine's clothes when she was a child, Mary did not take up quilting until after she retired. "Being of German descent, she was the hardest worker that I've ever known, and she loved learning new things," Elaine recalls. "Her philosophy of life (which she tried her best to teach me) was 'Use it up, wear it out, make it do, or do without!' That's why her quilts were scraps from her sewing, pieces from neighbors, and from my old high school dresses. In this particular quilt, she artistically designed each flower with a solid center, surrounded by whatever pattern the fabric bore. I enjoy pointing out my high school dresses to my friends. The quilt brings back many memories of my mom, and I cherish it!"[1]

Mary Hornseth and her daughter
Elaine Graber

Grandmother's Flower Garden, Mary Hornseth, 1980, MHQP 07-215-01 (98" x 98", cotton, blends)

THE Fort Peck Tribal Archives donated this bold Morning Star quilt, made by an unknown Indian artist, to the Montana Historical Society in memory of Sioux leader Gerald Red Elk and in honor of the Assiniboine and Sioux people.

While Montana quilters have for the most part quilted in accordance with national trends, quilts made by Montana's Indian peoples represent a unique regional art form. Long before they became quilters, Northern Plains Indians were skilled textile workers, adorning clothing and moccasins first with quills and later with beads. In the nineteenth century, Christian missionaries taught Plains Indians women to sew and quilt in the Euro-American way. Although quilting was intended to help Indian women acculturate, the women instead took up quiltmaking as a new medium for ancient arts and a way to continue old spiritual traditions. Nowhere is this cultural continuity more evident than in the Morning Star quilt.

Presbyterian ladies aid groups supposedly brought the Star quilt pattern to the Dakotas. From there it was introduced to Montana in the early twentieth century, although it is unclear by whom. According to anthropologist Nancy Tucker, Nellie Clark brought the Star quilt pattern back to the Fort Peck Reservation after she attended a Presbyterian school in South Dakota. Another account suggests that Nina First of Fort Kipp, a small community on the reservation, returned with the Star pattern after she served at a church mission in South Dakota in the 1920s. Lorena Shields believes her mother Louise Red Lightning introduced the Star quilt to Fort Peck when she relocated from South Dakota in 1926.

Whether she first introduced the pattern, Louise can certainly be credited for spreading the popularity of quiltmaking among the women of Fort Peck. A minister's wife, Louise taught the women of the ladies aid group to quilt in Reverend Red Lightning's tiny Presbyterian church in Fort Kipp.

Plains Indian women embraced the Star pattern in part because it resembled two sacred symbols: the morning star, the body that ushers in the new day and evokes the light of knowledge, and the circle, a sacrosanct form that represents the earth and the cycles of life. A circle with radiating points is a very old Indian design that used to be painted on buffalo robes. By the time the Star quilt form traveled to Montana, the buffalo had all but disappeared and Star quilts became a new way to continue the tradition. Color schemes in Native American Star quilts are also influenced by tradition. "Color choices often reflect the Native quilter's close spiritual ties to the natural world," points out quilt historian Marsha MacDowell. "Morning Star quilts are usually done in shades of blue—the color of the sky on cold winter mornings."[2]

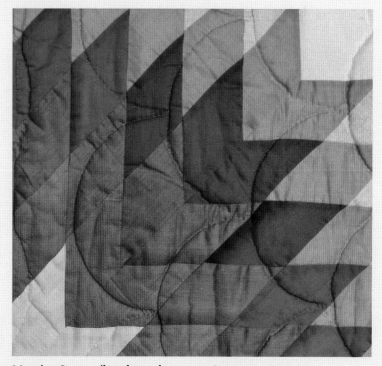

Morning Star, quiltmaker unknown, 1985, MHS 1985.92.01 (72" x 84", cotton/polyester)

In God, Liberty, and Freedom We Trust

SHIRLEY BARRETT

1986

SHIRLEY Barrett of Lakeside came up with this original design for the Great American Quilt Festival, a 1986 national competition sponsored in part by the Museum of American Folk Art to commemorate the Statue of Liberty's centennial. Barrett's *In God, Liberty, and Freedom We Trust* was chosen as Montana's finalist for the contest, and the quilt joined forty-nine other state finalists and two territorial finalists in a two-year, international traveling exhibition. The quilt was also featured in the book *All Flags Flying: American Patriotic Quilts as Expressions of Liberty* and won first place in Kalispell's quilt show and fair.

Shirley had been making quilts for five years when she tackled the subject of Lady Liberty. When asked about the reference she used for her depiction of the famous statue, Shirley explained, "[It's] the first quilt I've made where I had to use the encyclopedia and check out books from the library, only to discover that the best picture of 'the Lady' was right on my husband's baseball cap."[3]

(top) Shirley Barrett and Marjorie Sanders, chosen first and second, respectively, to represent Montana for the Statue of Liberty's centennial

(bottom) Shirley Barrett

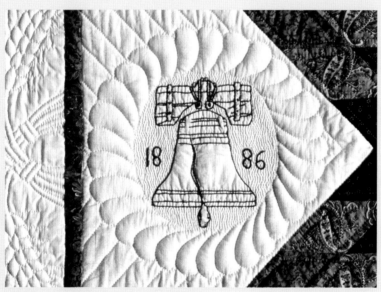

In God, Liberty, and Freedom We Trust, *Shirley Barrett, 1986,* MHQP 7-103-14 (70" x 71", cotton)

1889 MONTANA 1989

IN the past, quilting has been associated primarily with women, but there is historical evidence that men sewed and quilted as well. An article in the *Helena Independent Record* published during the 1949 Montana State Fair proclaimed: "Don't laugh, fellows; this may still be wild country, but men are doing fancy embroidery." That year, in contrast to the very masculine rodeo being held on the grounds, a glass cabinet in the Women's Building was dedicated entirely to *man*made fancy work. "Just in case you're snickering," the author chided, "everything entered by the men in the handicraft line is worthy of a blue ribbon."[4]

As quilts became perceived as a serious artistic medium in the 1970s and 1980s, it was no longer a laughing matter when men sat down at the sewing machine. Charles Rorvik, a retired engineering geologist and artist from Kalispell, decided to experiment with the form to commemorate Montana's centennial in 1989. Inspired by the paintings of cowboy artist Charles M. Russell and the wide-open scenery of the Sun River Valley, where his parents homesteaded, Charles used the construction principles he learned building dams to create his first and only quilt, which meant that he basically put the quilt together in reverse. He constructed the back first, then made the border. He finished by stitching the front. The batting is a wool army blanket from World War II. The quilt took Charles about a month to make, and he worked on it while taking care of his elderly parents in Choteau.

Charles "Chuck" Rorvik at work on a painting in his Kalispell home

Buffalo on the Range with Eagle and Buffalo Skull, *Charles Rorvik, 1989,* MHQP 07-268-02 *(81" x 101", polyester, velour, imitation fur)*

A Page from Great Falls Album, Falls Quilt Guild, 1989, MHQP 02-01-05 (82" x 83", cotton, blends)

MONTANA'S centennial in 1989 inspired quiltmakers across the state. The members of the Falls Quilt Guild commemorated one hundred years of statehood with this striking appliqué quilt. The blocks depict the people and places that formed Great Falls's rich history and culture, from explorers Meriwether Lewis and William Clark to Malmstrom Air Force Base to the Great Northern Railway. Organized by Penny Rubner and Pam Marlen, *A Page from Great Falls Album* was constructed and quilted by more than twenty guild members.

The guild members entered this quilt in a contest sponsored by the Montana Historical Society and were honored when it received a third place award. While on display at the Paris Gibson Square Museum of Art in Great Falls, the quilt was damaged when water pipes broke and the building flooded. The guild decided not to clean or restore the quilt because the water damage is now a part of the quilt's history. Fortunately, the quilt is in remarkably good shape, although faint signs of water damage can be seen on some blocks.

Falls Quilt Guild members Marge Sande and Penny Rubner with the quilt

This example of a commemorative quilt celebrates the one hundredth anniversary of the Montana Wool Growers. Montana Wool Growers Women, 1983, MHS 1984.59.01 (80" x 80", wool)

Star, Vera Bird Big Talk, 1992, MHQP 36-14-01 (73" x 82", polyester blends)

TODAY Plains Indian Star quilts are perhaps best known for their role in giveaways, traditional ceremonies in which an individual or family bestows food and gifts on others as a way of paying tribute to someone or commemorating a special event. Star quilts are among the most honored gifts at a giveaway, and the Sioux and Assiniboine of Montana's Fort Peck Reservation have put a contemporary spin on the traditional ceremony by bequeathing quilts at high school basketball tournaments.

According to historians C. Kurt Dewhurst and Marsha L. MacDowell, the genesis of the basketball-tournament quilt giveaway can be traced to an Indian custom for honoring warriors: "The basketball *star* quilt ceremony [comes from] an act of honoring at a 1947, Brockton, Montana, basketball game. Tessie Four Times, grandmother of one of the players, expressed her pride in her grandson by wiping the sweat from his back with a shawl and then casting the shawl on the floor for anyone to pick up. This act can be traced to a native custom of honoring those in battle. Years later, during discussions at a Red Eagle Presbyterian Ladies Aid Society meeting in early 1964, it was suggested to again honor Brockton players in this way. Along with other women in the community, the group began making *star* quilts in preparation for a giveaway at an upcoming game."[5] At that year's Class 2C District Tournament in Sidney, members of the Brockton Warriors gave the quilts to coaches and respected players on the other teams, and the tradition of honoring opponents with Star quilts has continued ever since.

Vera Bird Big Talk made this Star quilt in 1992 when the Brockton Warriors qualified for the Montana Class C Boys State Basketball Tournament. Vera painted the basketballs and the central player—William Conklin, a senior for the Warriors—with embroidery paints. Willie's family and friends, including several high school boys, helped Vera with the quilting. The quilt was presented to Stanford basketball player Christian Jette at the Class C State Tournament in Bozeman.

VERA BIRD BIG TALK

1992

Vera Bird Big Talk, at the urging of her grandson William "Georgie" Big Talk, created the two Star quilts hanging behind her. In 2002 she presented them to the mayors of New York and Washington, D.C., to show compassion and concern for those affected by the events of September 11, 2001. Georgie is pictured in the photograph she is holding.

Basketball is so important to Fort Peck Indian Reservation communities that Sioux quilters often give away Star quilts at tournaments. In February 2007 Jaylan Blount of Frazer (in black shirt) gave this Star quilt to Michael Crandel of Scobey (with quilt on his shoulders) as an act of friendship, even though the two played on opposing teams.

Montana Cartwheel, *Employees of the Quilt Gallery, 1992*, MHQP 15-06-01 *(80" x 96", cotton)*

Montana Cartwheel

JOAN Hodgeboom and Judy Niemeyer collaborated to design this dynamic, vividly colored quilt, which they named *Montana Cartwheel*. Joan, who learned to sew as a young woman in Massachusetts, brought her skills to Kalispell in 1980 when she moved there with her husband Fred. She started teaching sewing classes at a local fabric store, and when the owner moved in 1985, Joan took over the store, renamed it the Quilt Gallery, and began focusing exclusively on quiltmaking.

Judy says that she preferred milking cows to tying quilts as a child, but as a mother she made quilts for a living so she could stay home and be with her children. Around 1990 Judy began teaching classes at the Quilt Gallery, and Joan recalls how the two started designing quilts together: "The students would bring in an idea for a quilt and I would draw it up. Judy would help with construction. Judy then realized that her oldest son, Bradley, could do the drawing by computer."[6] *Montana Cartwheel* is a variation on their first pattern, *Montana Roundup*. Joan's shop continues to serve the quilters in the Flathead Valley, and Judy sells her patterns online.

Quiltmakers (standing, left to right): Judy Niemeyer, Joan Hodgeboom, Sharon Logan, Yvonne Kleinhaus; and (seated, left to right) "OK Carol" Rockwell and Caroline Kreps. Not pictured: Sheryl Mycroft

Green Hills
for Scottie

SHELLY VAN HAUR

1995

SHELLY Van Haur of Hilger is a Montana version of a renaissance woman. A teacher, rancher, and textile artist, Shelly began sewing around the age of five, helped her grandmother piece quilt tops by the time she was ten, and has been making quilts ever since.

In the mid-1990s, Shelly's skills as a quilter were so respected that she was chosen by the Montana Arts Council Folklife Program to teach a quiltmaking apprenticeship program to a handful of Hilger women. The group met in the old Hilger schoolhouse, and Shelly recalls their first winter in the building: "Almost every day... involved me getting there at 7:30 A.M. to shovel snow off the dreaded 75 feet of sidewalk, opening the outhouse door and getting the building heated up before anyone else got there. The community group in charge of the upkeep for the school could not afford to heat the building through the winter, so the plumbing had to be drained each fall before the first cold spell. We were using so much electricity for five sewing machines, irons, two floor dairy heaters and the lights that we constantly popped the breakers! You can't imagine trying to find a breaker box in a black basement using only farmer matches."[7]

Although Shelly spends much of her time quilting with others, she stitched *Green Hills for Scottie* by herself for her friend Scottie Byerly of Lewistown. The mountain scene was inspired by a photograph of the Gallatin National Forest near Bozeman.

Shelly Van Haur

Green Hills for Scottie, *Shelly Van Haur*, 1995, MHQP 08-109-02 (75" x 75", cotton)

Indian Orange Peel

KRISTI BILLMAYER
1996

KRISTI Billmayer hand-dyed the fabrics for this quilt, *Indian Orange Peel*, which is foundation-pieced from a pattern designed by Texas quilt designer Karen Stone that won the People's Choice Award at the 1995 Quilt National, an exhibition of contemporary art quilts that takes place each year in Athens, Ohio. Kristi tackled the *Indian Orange Peel* in 1996, and her quilt won first place for a large wall hanging that year in the Havre Hi-Line Quilt Guild Show and the quilter's award at the 1998 Montana Seed Show in Harlem.

Kristi lives on a ranch in Hogeland, a small community in northern Blaine County. The Wing Road Farm, which is managed by Kristi's husband Larry and his brother Gene, is a source of inspiration for Kristi, who makes her living as a painter and primarily works with pastels. Several of her paintings feature the ranch's dogs and horses. Her work has been honored with the People's Choice Award for Painting at the C. M. Russell Art Show and Auction in Great Falls.

Kristi Billmayer

(left) Indian Orange Peel, *Kristi Billmayer, 1996,* MHQP 24-02-04 *(62" x 62", cotton)*

(above) Orange Peel (also called Bay Leaf), *Lucy Jane Kemp Hyer Spracklin, 1932,* MHS 1997.86.02 *(detail, 38" x 55", cotton). This is a more traditional rendition of the Orange Peel or Bay Leaf pattern.*

Story Cloth of Missoula, *members of the Missoula Hmong American community, 1992–1993, Montana Museum of Art & Culture 00.01.07 (61" x 91", cotton)*

Story Cloth of Missoula

MEMBERS OF THE
MISSOULA HMONG
AMERICAN COMMUNITY

1992–1993

A RELATIVELY new contribution to the state's needlework traditions comes from the Hmong (pronounced "mung") who immigrated to Montana from Southeast Asia. Many of these Hmong had been recruited by the CIA to fight against Communist forces in the Laotian Civil War of 1962–1975, and when the Royal Lao government fell to the Communists in 1975, thousands were forced into refugee camps in Thailand. Having for centuries embellished their clothing with fine needlework, including appliqué, reverse appliqué, cross-stitch, and embroidery, they began producing *paj ntaub* (pronounced "pon dow"), or flower cloth, in the camps. Story-telling cloth (*pha pra vet*), a commercial type of paj ntaub, depicted narratives of traditional tales, Hmong daily and ceremonial life, and the experiences of war, migration, and resettlement.

In Montana the Hmong have continued to produce fine needlework. The story cloth pictured at left and right, *Story Cloth of Missoula*, was commissioned for a 1992–1993 Missoula Museum of the Arts exhibit on Hmong culture. A committee of Hmong volunteers decided what scenes to depict, and twelve-year-old art student Kou Moua and his father Yee Moua drew the subjects chosen. Mee Yang and Ia Vang, who had learned embroidery in Thailand before arriving in Missoula in the late 1980s, embroidered the cloth, and expert paj ntaub maker Nou Yang pieced the diamonds and borders and finished the cloth. Scenes include the airport, neighborhoods, schools, the university, and traditional Hmong activities, including growing vegetable gardens. Also pictured is the funeral of Jerry Daniels, a former Missoula smokejumper who served as a CIA operative in Laos and after the war worked passionately to help resettle Hmong refugees.

Celebration of Lewis and Clark

LIBBY DU BOIS PETTIT

2003

LIBBY Du Bois Pettit, a Missoula teacher and textile artist, made this quilt to commemorate the bicentennial of Meriwether Lewis and William Clark's exploration of the American Northwest. As Libby explains, "The quilt was designed and made from a Centennial Plate my mother, Rose Dow Du Bois, of Cookeville, Tennessee, bought in Kansas City, Missouri, for $5.00 in October of 1946. She loved it because she was born in 1905, the year the plate was made. In 1973 she gave me the plate because I was moving to Helena, Montana."[8]

The plate and the quilt now reside in Libby's home, which is situated along the banks of the Clark Fork River, a tributary of the Columbia River named after William Clark and explored by Meriwether Lewis during the expedition's 1806 return trip from the Pacific.

Libby Pettit and her granddaughters (left to right) Maria, Lia, and Emma Medley, 2008

(left) Celebration of Lewis and Clark, *Libby Du Bois Pettit, 2003,* MHQP 04-93-01 *(52" x 55", cotton)*

(above) *Pettit's depiction of the centennial plate from the "signature" block*

MONTANA'S rich history offers raw material for today's quilters, and the Hi-Line Quilt Guild of Havre has found particular inspiration in the everyday lives of Montana women. Suzanne Huston, an artist and quilt-maker, designed the blocks for *Petticoats and Prairies* using as her models historic photographs of frontier women mothering, baking, ironing, and horseback riding.

Suzanne based many of her blocks on the photographs of Evelyn Cameron, who was born to an upper-class English family in 1868 but moved with her husband Ewen to the plains of eastern Montana in the 1890s. The couple settled on a ranch south of Terry, where Cameron's life on the prairie was a far cry from her genteel upbringing. She took in boarders, raised and sold vegetables, and cooked for roundup crews to make extra money. After her husband died in 1915, she ran the ranch alone for thirteen years.

Cameron also taught herself photography with a mail-order five-by-seven-inch Graflex. She took thousands of pictures documenting her daily life, but her work was largely unknown when she passed away in 1928. In the 1970s, however, Donna Lucey began poking through the basement of Terry resident Janet Williams, who had been one of Cameron's best friends and had kept thousands of her negatives and photographic prints as well as letters, manuscripts, and diaries. Lucey brought national attention to Cameron's work with the 1990 publication of *Photographing Montana, 1894–1928: The Life and Work of Evelyn Cameron.* Easily one of Montana's most inspirational women, Cameron herself appears in *Petticoats and Prairies,* on the second block from the bottom on the far left (and detailed below).

The Hi-Line Quilt Guild made *Petticoats and Prairies* to raise money to bring national quilt teachers to Havre, but the guild also gives back to the community by providing sewing supplies to area schools and donating time and money to local 4-H groups.

Suzanne Huston, who designed this quilt, also designed and made the Puerto Rican Christmas Parade that appears at the beginning of this chapter.

Petticoats and Prairies, *Hi-Line Quilt Guild, 2002,* MHQP 12-08-01 *(94" x 98", cotton)*

"Evelyn Kneading a panful of dough in her kitchen, August 1904"

Notes

PREFACE

1. Henry Glassie, "Meaningful Things and Appropriate Myths: The Artifact's Place in American Studies," in *Material Life in America, 1600–1860*, ed. Robert Blair St. George (Boston: Northeastern University Press, 1998), 82.

INTRODUCTION

The author would like to thank Joan Jensen and Dale Martin for their careful reading of this essay and very helpful suggestions. Jodi Rasker, Sue Armitage, Don Beld, Joseph Miller Jr., and Jim Ward were generous with their time and provided critical research. The Montana State University College of Letters & Science provided critical research funds.

1. Mirra Bank, *Anonymous Was a Woman* (New York: St. Martin's, 1979); Patricia Mainardi, "Quilts: The Great American Art," *Feminist Art Journal* 2 (Winter 1973): 1, 18–23; Patsy and Myron Orlofsky, *Quilts in America* (1974; repr., New York: Abbeville Press, 1992); Roderick Kiracofe, *The American Quilt: A History of Cloth and Comfort, 1750–1950* (New York: Clarkson Potter, 1993); Janet Catherine Berlo and Patricia Cox Crews, *Wild by Design: Two Hundred Years of Innovation and Artistry in American Quilts* (Lincoln, Neb., and Seattle: International Quilt Study Center in association with University of Washington Press, 2003).

2. Laura Heine, *Color Fusion* (Columbus, Ohio: Dragon Threads, 2001), 6.

3. Information on Susan Newcomer's quilt is in the collection files of the Museum of the Rockies, Bozeman, Montana. See the obituaries of Amanda (March 3, 1931), Elden (September 17, 1959), and Hazel (August 17, 1967) in the *Winnett (Mont.) Times*. For Hazel's career, see John A. Forssen, ed., *Petticoat and Stethoscope: A Montana Legend* (Missoula, Mont.: Bitterroot Litho, 1978), 14.

4. Barbara Brackman, "Quilts on the Kansas Frontier," *Kansas History* 13 (Spring 1990): 13–22. Brackman's conclusions are documented in other studies, for example, Patricia Cox Crews and Ronald C. Naugle, eds., *Nebraska Quilts and Quiltmakers* (Lincoln: University of Nebraska Press, 1991); Nancyann Johnson Twelker, *Women and Their Quilts: A Washington State Centennial Tribute* (Bothell, Wash.: That Patchwork Place, 1988); and Mary Bywater Cross, *Quilts of the Oregon Trail* (Atglen, Pa.: Schiffer, 2007).

5. See U.S. census for general statistics. Sex ratios for 1910 are found in U.S. Bureau of the Census, *Thirteenth Census of the United States Taken in the Year 1910, vol. II, Population, 1910, Reports by States, Alabama-Montana* (Washington, D.C.: Government Printing Office, 1913), 1145. General population figures for 1870–1910 are in ibid., 1132.

6. May G. Flanagan, "Personal Recollections," in *Our Fort Benton of Yesterday and Today*, ed. Nora E. Harber (Fort Benton, Mont.: River Press, n.d.), 13.

7. Anita B. Loscalzo, "The History of the Sewing Machine and Its Use in Quilting in the United States," *Uncoverings* 26 (2005): 175–208; Elizabeth M. Bacon, "Marketing Sewing Machines in the Post-Civil War Years," *Bulletin of the Business Historical Society* 20 (June 1946): 90–94.

8. David Blanke, "A Comparison of the Catalogs Issued from Sears, Roebuck & Company and Montgomery Ward & Company, 1893–1906," *Essays in Economic and Business History, Selected Papers from the Economic and Business Historical Society* 12 (1994): 328; Louis E. Asher and Edith Heal, *Send No Money* (Chicago: Argus, 1942), 77, 55.

9. Thomas J. Schlereth, "Country Stores, County Fairs, and Mail-order Catalogues: Consumption in Rural America," in *Consuming Visions: Accumulation and Display of Goods in America, 1880–1920*, ed. Simon J. Broner (New York: W.W. Norton, 1989), 369–70; Marguerite Connolly, "The Disappearance of the Domestic Sewing Machine, 1890–1925," *Winterthur Portfolio* 34 (Spring 1999): 37.

10. Grace Stoddard Mason Letters, SC 1699, Montana Historical Society Research Center, Helena (hereafter MHS). All quotations from Grace are from these letters. Grace usually dated her letters with vague headings like, "Monday afternoon 1913," so I have not listed specific dates for each quotation, but for anyone searching for a particular letter, the collection is not large.

11. Ibid. On Culbertson's development, see *Culbertson Diamond Jubilee 1887–1972, Seventy-Five Years of Progress* (Culbertson, Mont., 1962); and Loretta Segars, *One Hundred Years in Culbertson, 1887–1987* (n.p., 1986). Laurann Gilbertson, "Patterns of the New World: Quiltmaking among Norwegian Americans," *Uncoverings* 27 (2006): 157–96, discusses the variety of ways immigrants to the northern plains obtained fabric. Cynthia Culver Prescott in *Gender and Generation on the Far Western Frontier* (Tucson: University of Arizona Press, 2007) has an excellent discussion of the changing trends and increasing importance of clothing and quilting as a more developed consumer society emerged in the West.

12. Grace Stoddard Mason Letters, MHS.

13. Folders 1 and 2, box 4, Helena Woman's Club Records, MC 303, MHS.

14. Quoted in Douglas M. Edwards, "Fair Days in the 'Zone of Plenty': Exhibit Networks and the Development of the American West" (PhD diss., University of Maryland, 2001), 51; Board of World's Fair Managers of the State of Montana, *Proceedings of Board of World's Fair Managers* (Helena, Mont.: C. K. Wells, 1892), 82.

15. *Proceedings of Board of World's Fair Managers,* 82–83, 84; Barbara Brackman, "Quilts at Chicago's World's Fairs," *Uncoverings* 2 (1981): 65. Brackman found another list that included four other quilts but without any accompanying information as to their origins.

16. Edwards, "Fair Days," 148; The Thirteenth Annual Premium List of the M.A.M. and M.A., 1882, MHS.

17. For annual fairs, see the collection of "Premium List, Rules & Regulations for the Montana Agricultural, Mineral and Mechanical Association," MHS.

18. Ibid.

19. Edwards, "Fair Days," 128; Douglas M. Edwards, "Exhibiting the Possibilities: The Montana State Fair" (master's thesis, Montana State University, 1997), 78; Virginia Gunn, "Quilts at Nineteenth Century State and County Fairs: An Ohio Study," *Uncoverings* 9 (1988): 106.

20. Karal Ann Marling, *Blue Ribbon: A Social and Pictorial History of the Minnesota State Fair* (St. Paul: Minnesota Historical Society Press, 1990), 96–97; Montana State Fair premium lists, 1903–1931, MHS.

21. Merikay Waldvogel and Barbara Brackman, *Patchwork Souvenirs of the 1933 World's Fair: The Sears National Quilt Contest and Chicago's Century of Progress Exposition* (Nashville, Tenn.: Rutledge Hill, 1993), 35, 10, 115.

22. See the collection of "State Course of Study," 1910s–1942, MHS. Sewing lessons are enumerated in the *Handbook to Accompany Course of Study for Rural Schools of Montana* (n.p., September 1917).

23. Nancy H. Tucker, *Indian Star Quilts: Women in Transition* (Ware, Mass.: Mary S. & Niles Tucker, 1999), 56, 57; Lotta Allen Meacham, "The Crow Indian Fair," *Independent* 65 (September 18, 1908): 656–57.

24. *The Iapi Oaye, The Word Carrier* 5, no. 5 (May 1876); ibid., vol. 2, no. 1 (January 1873); Tucker, *Indian Star Quilts,* 61.

25. *Word Carrier,* n.s., vol. 2, no. 8, 9, 10 (October, November, December 1885).

26. Tucker, *Indian Star Quilts,* 21. The Garfield quilt is held by the Denver Museum of Nature and Science. All information comes from its files, object AC.2002. For information on James Garfield Sr., see Joe McGeschick et al., *The History of the Assiniboine and Sioux Tribes of the Fort Peck Indian Reservation, Montana, 1800–2000* (Helena: Fort Peck Community College and Montana Historical Society Press, 2008). Joseph Miller Jr., James Garfield's grandnephew, recalled hearing a story about a woman who hanged herself and that "the tree used to be standing and people who passed by knew of the story and would recount it." Email correspondence with author, April 6, 2008.

27. Patricia Albers and Beatrice Medicine, "The Role of Sioux Women in the Production of Ceremonial Objects: The Case of the Star Quilt," in *The Hidden Half: Studies of Plains Indian Women,* ed. Patricia Albers and Beatrice Medicine (Washington, D.C.: University Press of America, 1988), 123–40; Jeanne Eder, *My Grandmother's Star Quilt Honors Me* exhibition program, Western Heritage Center, Billings, Montana, 1987.

28. Jeanne Field Olson, "Love in Every Stitch: Quilting in Montana," *Montana Magazine,* November–December 1996, 21; Florence Pulford, *Morning Star Quilts: A Presentation of the Work and Lives of Northern Plains Indian Women* (Los Altos, Calif.: Leone, 1989), 66, 79.

29. Albers and Medicine, "Role of Sioux Women," 129–34; Marsha L. MacDowell and C. Kurt Dewhurst, eds., *To Honor and Comfort: Native Quilting Traditions* (Santa Fe: Museum of New Mexico and Michigan State University Museum, 1997), 51–54.

30. Linnie White Greathouse, "Montana Memories," typescript in possession of author, 46–47.

31. T. M. Pearce, "Three Rocky Mountain Terms: Park, Sugan, and Plaza," *American Speech* 33 (May 1958): 104–5; Lois Flansburg Haaglund, *Tough, Willing, and Able: Tales of a Montana Family* (Missoula, Mont.: Mountain Press, 1997), 2–4.

32. The poem is a typescript in folder 12, box 5, T. O. Larson Papers, MC 307, MHS. I quote from the published version in Johnny Ritch, *Horsefeathers* (Helena, Mont.: Naegele Printing, 1940), 55–71.

33. Kenneth D. Swan, *Splendid Was the Trail* (Missoula, Mont.: Mountain Press, 1968), 46.

34. Sarah J. Tracy journal, Museum of the Rockies, Bozeman, Montana.

35. Dorothy Cozart, in "A Century of Fundraising Quilts: 1860–1960," *Uncoverings* 5 (1984): 41–53, found that churches were the beneficiaries of most of the fund-raising quilts she could document.

36. Rev. Alice Barnes Hoag and Mrs. Matthew W. Alderson, *Historical Sketch of the Montana Woman's Christian Temperance Union, 1883–1912* (Helena, Mont.: State Publishing, 1912).

37. Miss Alice Nichols, a Quaker, had been at the founding of the Montana WCTU and she remained a dedicated organizer throughout her life, serving as president, treasurer, state organizer, editor of the union's publications, and national and international delegate. Miss Nichols married H. H. Barnes, and at some point she also became Reverend Alice Barnes and served for a time as pastor of the Congregational church in Columbus. For the history of the quilt given her at the 1902 convention, see "Minutes of the 19th Annual Convention of Montana WCTU, Sept. 23–25, 1902, Butte," folder 1, box 9, Montana Woman's Christian Temperance Union Records, 1883–1976, MC 160, MHS; and Hoag and Alderson, *Historical Sketch.*

38. Nancy J. Rowley, "Red Cross Quilts for the Great War," *Uncoverings* 3 (1982): 44; W. W. Gail, ed., *Yellowstone County Montana in the World War, 1917–1918–1919* (Billings, Mont.: War Book Publishing, 1919), 174, 178.

39. On the Red Cross quilt, see documents file, X82.71.01, Montana Historical Society Museum, Helena. In 2004, a group of volunteers from the Friends of the Montana

Historical Society made a replica of the Red Cross quilt as a fundraiser for the Intermountain Children's Home.

40. Barbara Brackman, *Quilts from the Civil War* (Lafayette, Calif., C&T, 1997), chap. 4; Virginia Gunn, "Quilts for Civil War Soldiers from Peacham, Vermont," *Uncoverings* 22 (2001): 50. Barbara

41. Florence Fisk White, "The Autograph Quilt," folder 2, box 4, Fisk Family Papers, MC 31, MHS (hereafter Fisk Papers).

42. R. Emmett Fisk to Fannie Chester, September 18, 1864, folder 13, box 4, Fisk Papers.

43. Lizzie Chester to Capt. R. E. Fisk, October 3, 1864, folder 14, box 9, Fisk Papers.

44. A selection of Robert's and Lizzie's letters that detail their life in Montana is in Rex C. Myers, ed., *Lizzie: The Letters of Elizabeth Chester Fisk, 1864–1893* (Missoula, Mont.: Mountain Press, 1989).

45. Ibid., 80, 88.

46. White, "The Autograph Quilt"; Don Beld, emails to author, February 15, 16, 2008. The Fisk quilt is now in the collections of the Redlands Library, Redlands, California.

CHAPTER ONE

1. Susan Badger Doyle, ed., *Bound for Montana: Diaries from the Bozeman Trail* (Helena: Montana Historical Society Press, 2004), 114.

2. Ibid., 120.

3. Elaine Hedges, *Hearts and Hands: Women, Quilts, and American Society* (1987; repr., Nashville, Tenn.: Rutledge Hill, 1996), 52, 54.

4. Michael P. Malone, Richard B. Roeder, and William L. Lang, *Montana: A History of Two Centuries*, rev. ed. (Seattle: University of Washington Press, 1991), 171.

5. Barbara Welter, "The Cult of True Womanhood," *American Quarterly* 18, no. 2 (Summer 1966): 152.

6. Hedges, *Hearts and Hands*, 26–27.

7. Paul Ballinger Davidson, "Florence Ballinger Hamilton, 1873–1970," courtesy Jane Klockman, copy in Collection 2488, Hamilton, Ballinger, Davidson, Bunnell, McAfee, and Weesner Family Papers, 1764–1998, Merrill G. Burlingame Special Collections, Montana State University Libraries, Bozeman.

8. Virginia M. Fox, letter to author, March 14, 2007.

9. Ibid.

10. Sue Lepley, email to author, March 11, 2008.

11. Jacqueline L. Tobin and Raymond G. Dobard, *Hidden in Plain View: A Secret Story of Quilts and the Underground Railroad* (New York: Doubleday, 1999); Barbara Brackman, *Facts and Fabrications: Unraveling the History of Quilts and Slavery* (LaFayette, Calif.: C&T, 2006), 7.

12. Eileen Jahnke Trestain, *Dating Fabrics: A Color Guide, 1800–1960* (Paducah, Ky.: American Quilter's Society, 1998), 194.

13. Tom Stout, ed., *Montana, Its Story and Biography: A History of Aboriginal and Territorial Montana and Three Decades of Statehood*, vol. 2 (Chicago: American Historical Society, 1921), 53–54.

14. Barbara Brackman, "Nineteenth-century Album Patterns," *Quilters Newsletter Magazine*, July-August 1990, 21.

15. Geraldine Torske, interview by Sandra Weaver, May 7,

1987, copy of transcript in folder 1-6, box 1, MC 17, Montana Historic Quilt Project Records, Montana Historical Society Research Center and Archives, Helena (hereafter MC 17, MHS).

16. Linda Peavy and Ursula Smith, *The Gold Rush Widows of Little Falls: A Story Drawn from the Letters of Pamelia and James Fergus* (St. Paul: Minnesota Historical Society Press, 1990), 161.

CHAPTER TWO

1. Michael P. Malone, Richard B. Roeder, and William L. Lang, *Montana: A History of Two Centuries*, rev. ed. (Seattle: University of Washington Press, 1991), 236.

2. Mary Murphy, *Hope in Hard Times: New Deal Photographs of Montana, 1936–1942* (Helena: Montana Historical Society Press, 2003), 27.

3. Seena B. Kohl, "'Well I have lived in Montana almost a week and like it fine': Letters from the Davis Homestead, 1910–1926," *Montana The Magazine of Western History* 51 (Autumn 2001): 40.

4. Elaine Hedges, *Hearts and Hands: Women, Quilts, and American Society* (1987; repr., Nashville, Tenn.: Rutledge Hill, 1996), 37; Thomas K. Woodward and Blanche Greenstein, *Twentieth Century Quilts, 1900–1950* (New York: E. P. Dutton, 1988), 7.

5. *Helena (Mont.) Daily Independent*, May 15, 1874.

6. Ibid., June 13, 28, 1874; *Butte (Mont.) Miner*, November 7, 1876.

7. *Helena (Mont.) Daily Independent*, June 8, 1876, February 11, 1875.

8. Nancy J. Rowley, "Red Cross Quilts for the Great War," *Uncoverings* 3 (1982): 44, quoting Cuesta Benberry, "The 20th Century's First Quilt Revival," *Quilter's Newsletter* 116 (October 1979).

9. *Helena (Mont.) Daily Independent*, June 22, 1932.

10. Ibid., January 16, 1977; *Billings (Mont.) Gazette*, May 1, 1975.

11. Belle Fligelman Winestine, quoted in Jeanne Abrams, *Jewish Women Pioneering the Frontier Trail: A History in the American West* (New York: New York University Press, 2006), 164.

12. *Freeport (Mich.) Freeport*, February 3, 1927.

13. Quoted in Lynn A. Bonfield, "The Production of Cloth, Cloth-ing and Quilts in 19th Century New England Homes," *Uncoverings* (1981): 83.

14. Barbara Brackman, "Quilts at Chicago's World's Fairs," *Uncoverings* 2 (1981), 66.

15. *Mary Ronan, Girl from the Gulches: The Story of Mary Ronan as Told to Margaret Ronan*, ed. Ellen Baumler (Helena: Montana Historical Society Press, 2003), 133.

16. *Great Falls (Mont.) Tribune*, April 18, 1965.

17. T. M. Pearce, "Three Rocky Mountain Terms: Park, Sugan, and Plaza," *American Speech* 33 (May 1958): 103.

18. Edna Mae Miller, interview by Sandra Weaver, May 5, 1987, transcript in folder 1–7, box 1, MC 17, Montana Historic Quilt Project Records, Montana Historical Society Research Center, Helena.

19. *Yesteryears and Pioneers: Wheatland County* (Harlowton, Mont.: Harlowton Woman's Club, 1972), 291.

20. Janet Catherine Berlo and Patricia Cox Crews, *Wild by Design: Two Hundred Years of Innovation and Artistry in American Quilts* (Lincoln, Neb.: International Quilt Study Center; Seattle: University of Washington Press, 2003), 72.

21. *Anaconda (Mont.) Standard*, July 7, 1909.

22. Ibid.

23. *Helena (Mont.) Daily Independent*, September 12, 1919.

24. *In the Years Gone By: Simpson, Cottonwood* (Cottonwood, Mont.: Cottonwood Home Demonstration Club, 1964), 170.

CHAPTER THREE

1. Mary Murphy, *Hope in Hard Times: New Deal Photographs of Montana, 1936–1942* (Helena: Montana Historical Society Press, 2003), 48.

2. Julia June Chitwood Trees, quoted in ibid., 61–62.

3. Quoted in Merikay Waldvogel, *Soft Covers for Hard Times: Quiltmaking and the Great Depression* (Nashville, Tenn.: Rutledge Hill, 1990), 2.

4. Anne Copeland and Beverly Dunivent, "Kit Quilts in Perspective," *Uncoverings* 15 (1994): 148.

5. Emma Louise Riley Smith, quoted in Quinard Taylor and Shirley Ann Wilson Moore, eds., *African American Women Confront the West, 1600–2000* (Norman: University of Oklahoma Press), 132.

6. Mildred K. Stoltz, *This Is Yours: The Montana Farmers Union and Its Cooperative Associates* (Minneapolis: Lund Press, 1956), 99.

7. Ibid., 100.

8. Barbara Brackman, *Clues in the Calico: A Guide to Identifying and Dating Antique Quilts* (Charlottesville, Va.: Howell Press, 1989), 169.

9. *Kalispell (Mont.) Daily Inter Lake*, August 15, 1976.

10. *Great Falls (Mont.) Tribune*, February 26, 1951.

11. *Helena (Mont.) Daily Independent*, May 17, 1923.

12. Marjorie Miner Solberg, "The Ossette Quilters," folder 6-2a, box 6, MC 17, Montana Historic Quilt Project Records, Montana Historical Society Research Center and Archives, Helena (hereafter Mc 17, MHS).

13. Kari Ronning, "'Love Was in the Work': Pieced Quilts," in *Nebraska Quilts and Quiltmakers*, ed. Patricia Cox Crews and Ronald C. Naugle (Lincoln: University of Nebraska Press, 1991), 64.

14. "Grandmother's Flower Garden Quilt," folder 12-10, box 12, MC 17, MHS.

15. Sandi Fox, *Small Endearments: Nineteenth-century Quilts for Children* (New York: Charles Scribner's Sons, 1985), 4.

16. Barbara Truckner to author, February 22, 2007.

17. Virginia Gunn, "Yo-Yo or Bed-of-Roses Quilts: Nineteenth Century Origins," *Uncoverings* 8 (1987): 135, 137.

18. Thomas K. Woodward and Blanche Greenstein, *Twentieth Century Quilts, 1900–1950* (New York: E. P. Dutton, 1988), 34.

19. Patricia Snapp, letter to author, March 2007.

20. Ibid.

CHAPTER FOUR

1. *Missoula (Mont.) Missoulian*, "A Salute to the Greatest Generation, part II," October 28, 2001, http://www.missoulian.com/specials/salute/Salute2-home.html.

2. Matthew Basso, "Man-Power: Montana Copper Workers, State Authority, and the (Re)drafting of Manhood during World War II," in *Across the Great Divide: Cultures of Manhood in the American West*, ed. Matthew Basso, Laura McCall, and Dee Garceau (New York: Routledge, 2001), 206.

3. Freddie Hopgood, "Under 'Drunkard's Pathway,'" *Billings (Mont.) Gazette*, December 15, 1968.

4. *Hardin (Mont.) Tribune*, January 1, 1909.

5. Margaret Jensen, assisted by Leila Williams, *Looking Back* (Denver: Big Mountain, 1966), 25, 43.

6. Ibid., 54.

7. *Billings Gazette*, March 12, 1990.

8. Helen Pease Wolf, *Reaching Both Ways* (Laramie, Wyo.: Jelm Mountain, 1989), 49.

9. Georgia Rae Easter, quoted in Marsha L. MacDowell, "North American Indian and Native Hawaiian Quiltmaking," in *To Honor and Comfort: Native Quilting Traditions*, ed. Marsha L. MacDowell and C. Kurt Dewhurst (Santa Fe: Museum of New Mexico Press, 1997), 19.

CHAPTER FIVE

1. Elaine Graber to Tonya Easbey, March 19, 2007, copy in possession of author.

2. Marsha MacDowell, "North American Indian and Native Hawaiian Quiltmaking," in *To Honor and Comfort: Native Quilting Traditions*, ed. Marsha L. McDowell and C. Kurt Dewhurst (Santa Fe: Museum of New Mexico Press qand Michigan State University Museum, 1997), 30.

3. Robert Bishop and Carter Houck, *All Flags Flying: American Patriotic Quilts as Expressions of Liberty* (New York: E. P. Dutton, 1986), 78.

4. *Helena (Mont.) Independent Record*, August 4, 1949.

5. C. Kurt Dewhurst and Marsha L. MacDowell, "Stars of Honor: The Basketball Star Quilt Ceremony," in MacDowell and Dewhurst, *To Honor and Comfort*, 132–33.

6. Joan Hodgeboom, letter to author, December 15, 2006.

7. Alexandra Swaney, ed., *From the Heart and Hand: Montana Folk and Traditional Arts Apprenticeships, 1992–1996* (Helena: Montana Folklife Program of the Montana Arts Council, 2001), 51.

8. Libby Du Bois Pettit, "Celebration of Lewis and Clark, 1803–2003," copy in possession of author.

Selected Bibliography

This list of sources includes the published works on Montana history, women's history, and quiltmaking that assisted in the research for this book.

Abrahams, Ethel Ewert, and Rachel K. Pannabecker. "'Better Choose Me': Addictions to Tobacco, Collecting, and Quilting, 1880–1920." *Uncoverings* 21 (2000): 79-105.

Abrams, Jeanne E. *Jewish Women Pioneering the Frontier Trail: A History in the American West.* New York: New York University Press, 2006.

Albers, Patricia, and Beatrice Medicine. "The Role of Sioux Women in the Production of Ceremonial Objects: The Case of the Star Quilt." In *The Hidden Half: Studies of Plains Indian Women.* Edited by Patricia Albers and Beatrice Medicine. Washington, D.C.: University Press of America, 1988.

Asher, Louis E., and Edith Heal. *Send No Money.* Chicago: Argus, 1942.

Atkins, Jacqueline M., and Phyllis A. Tepper. *New York Beauties.* New York: Dutton Studio Books, 1992.

Bacon, Elizabeth M. "Marketing Sewing Machines in the Post-Civil War Years." *Bulletin of the Business Historical Society* 20 (June 1946): 90–94.

Ballard, Debra. "The Ladies Aid of Hope Lutheran Church." *Uncoverings* 10 (1989): 69–80.

Bank, Mirra. *Anonymous Was a Woman.* New York: St. Martin's, 1979.

Basso, Matthew. "Man-Power: Montana Copper Workers, State Authority, and the (Re)drafting of Manhood during World War II." In *Across the Great Divide: Cultures of Manhood in the American West.* Edited by Matthew Basso, Laura McCall, and Dee Garceau, 185–210. New York: Routledge, 2001.

Benberry, Cuesta. "The Twentieth Century's First Quilt Revival." *Quilter's Newsletter,* no. 116 (October 1979).

Berlo, Janet, and Patricia Cox Crews. *Wild by Design: Two Hundred Years of Innovation and Artistry in American Quilts.* Lincoln, Neb.: International Quilt Study Center; Seattle: University of Washington Press, 2003.

Bishop, Robert, and Carter Houck. *All Flags Flying: American Patriotic Quilts as Expressions of Liberty.* New York: E. P. Dutton, 1986.

Blanke, David. "A Comparison of the Catalogs Issued from Sears, Roebuck & Company and Montgomery Ward & Company, 1893–1906." *Essays in Economic and Business History, Selected Papers from the Economic and Business Historical Society* 12 (1994): 328.

Bonfield, Lynn A. "The Production of Cloth, Clothing and Quilts in Nineteenth Century New England Homes." *Uncoverings* 2 (1981): 77–94.

———. "Quilts for Civil War Soldiers from Peacham, Vermont." *Uncoverings* 12 (2001): 37–64.

Brackman, Barbara, *Clues in the Calico: A Guide to Identifying and Dating Antique Quilts.* Charlottesville, Va.: Howell, 1989.

———. *Encyclopedia of Applique: An Illustrated, Numerical Index to Traditional and Modern Patterns.* McLean, Va.: EPM Publications, 1993.

———. *Encyclopedia of Pieced Quilt Patterns.* Paducah, Ky.: American Quilter's Society, 1993.

———. *Facts and Fabrications: Unraveling the History of Quilts and Slavery.* LaFayette, Calif.: C&T, 2006.

———. "Nineteenth-century Album Patterns." *Quilter's Newsletter Magazine,* July–August 1990, 20–23.

———. *Patterns of History, 1930–1950.* Kansas City, Mo.: Kansas City Star Books, 2004.

———. "Quiltmaking on the Overland Trails." *Uncoverings* 13 (1992): 45–60.

———. "Quilts at Chicago's World's Fairs." *Uncoverings* 2 (1981): 63–76.

———. *Quilts from the Civil War.* Lafayette, Calif.: C&T, 1997.

———. "Quilts on the Kansas Frontier." *Kansas History* 13 (Spring 1990): 13–22.

———. "Signature Quilts: Nineteenth Century Trends." *Uncoverings* 10 (1989): 25–37.

Brackman, Barbara, Jennie A. Chinn, Gayle R. Davis, Terry Thompson, Sara Reimer Farley, and Nancy Hornback. *Kansas Quilts and Quilters.* Lawrence: University of Kansas Press, 1993.

Bresenhan, Karoline Patterson, and Nancy O'Bryant Puentes. *Lone Stars.* Vol. 2, *A Legacy of Texas Quilts, 1936–1986.* Austin: University of Texas Press, 1990.

Carlson, Linda Giesler. *Roots, Feathers, and Blooms: 4-Block Quilts, Their History and Patterns.* Vol. 1. Paducah, Ky.: American Quilter's Society, 1994.

Cerny, Catherine A. "A Quilt Guild: Its Role in the Elaboration of Female Identity." *Uncoverings* 12 (1991): 33–49.

———. "Quilt Ownership and Sentimental Attachments: The Structure of Memory." *Uncoverings* 18 (1997): 95–119.

Cheney, Roberta Carkeek. *Names on the Face of Montana: The Story of Montana's Place Names.* Missoula, Mont.: Mountain Press, 1983.

Clark, Ricky. "Ruth Finley and the Colonial Revival Era." *Uncoverings* 16 (1995): 33–65.

Clawson, Roger. "Indian Star Quilts." *Lady's Circle Patchwork Quilts,* January 1993, 30–36.

Collins, Herbert Ridgeway. *Threads of History: Americana Recorded on Cloth, 1775 to the Present.* Washington, D.C.: Smithsonian Institution Press, 1979.

Connolly, Marguerite. "The Disappearance of the Domestic Sewing Machine, 1890–1925." *Winterthur Portfolio* 34 (Spring 1999): 37.

Copeland, Anne, and Beverly Dunivent. "Kit Quilts in Perspective." *Uncoverings* 15 (1994): 141–67.

Cord, Xenia E. "Marketing Quilt Kits in the 1920s and 1930s." *Uncoverings* 16 (1995): 141–72.

Cozart, Dorothy. "A Century of Fundraising Quilts: 1860–1960." *Uncoverings* 5 (1984): 41–53.

Crews, Patricia Cox, and Ronald C. Naugle, eds. *Nebraska Quilts and Quiltmakers.* Lincoln: University of Nebraska Press, 1991.

Cross, Mary Bywater. "The Anti-polygamy Quilt by the Ogden Methodist Quilting Bee." *Uncoverings* 24 (2003): 17–39.

———. *Quilts and Women of the Mormon Migrations.* Nashville, Tenn.: Rutledge Hill, 1996.

———. "Quilts in the Lives of Women Who Migrated in the Northwest, 1850–1990: A Visual Record Bywater." In *Women in Pacific Northwest History.* Edited by Karen J. Blair, 258–266. Rev. ed. Seattle: University of Washington Press, 2001.

———. *Quilts of the Oregon Trail.* Atglen, Pa.: Schiffer, 2007.

Culbertson Diamond Jubilee 1887–1972, Seventy-five Years of Progress. Culbertson, Mont., 1962.

Cummings, Patricia Lynne Grace. *Straight Talk about Quilt Care: Display, Cleaning, and Storage of New and Antique Quilts and Needlework.* Concord, N.H.: Quilter's Muse, 2005.

———. *Treasures in the Trunk: Quilts of the Oregon Trail.* Nashville, Tenn.: Rutledge Hill, 1993.

Dallas, Sandra. "Quilts Stitch a History of Women's Journey West." *Silver Queen Preservation* 35 (Fall 2004), http://www.historicgeorgetown.org/news/fa1104/newsfa1104.htm#articlelist.

Dallas, Sandra, and Nanette Simonds. *The Quilt That Walked to Golden: Women and Quilts in the Mountain West from the Overland Trail to Contemporary Colorado.* Elmhurst, Ill.: Breckling, 2004.

Davis, Marilyn. "The Contemporary American Quilter: A Portrait." *Uncoverings* 2 (1981): 45–51.

de Graaf, Lawrence B. "Race, Sex, and Region: Black Women in the American West, 1850–1920." *Pacific Historical Review* 49 (May 1980): 285–313.

Design Dynamics of Log Cabin Quilts: Selections from the Collection of Jonathan Holstein. Lincoln: International Quilt Study Center, University of Nebraska, http://www.quiltstudy.org/includes/downloads/galleryguide.pdf.

Dick, Carol, comp. *Hart to Hartt: A Family History.* N.p., n.d.

Dimock-Quaglia, Cynthia. "The 'Vampire' Quilt: A Material-Culture Study." *Uncoverings* 20 (1999): 159–83.

Doyle, Susan Badger, ed. *Bound for Montana: Diaries from the Bozeman Trail.* Helena: Montana Historical Society Press, 2004.

Eldredge, Charles C. "Museum News." *Art Journal* 39 (Spring 1980): 202–13.

Elsley, Judy. "The Smithsonian Quilt Controversy: Cultural Dislocation." *Uncoverings* 14 (1993): 119–36.

Federal Writers' Project of the Work Projects Administration for the State of Montana. *Montana: A State Guide Book.* New York: Viking, 1939.

Finley, Ruth E. *Old Patchwork Quilts and the Women Who Made Them.* Philadelphia: J. B. Lippincott Company, 1929.

Finn, Janet L., and Ellen Crain, eds. *Motherlode: Legacies of Women's Lives and Labors in Butte, Montana.* Livingston, Mont.: Clark City, 2005.

Flynn, John. "Montana's Quilting Engineer." *Lady's Circle Patchwork Quilts,* January 1993, 38–43.

Forssen, John A., ed. *Petticoat and Stethoscope: A Montana Legend.* Missoula, Mont.: Bitterroot Litho, 1978.

Fox, Sandi. *For Purpose and Pleasure: Quilting Together in Nineteenth-century America.* Nashville, Tenn.: Rutledge Hill, 1995.

———. *Small Endearments: Nineteenth-century Quilts for Children.* New York: Charles Scribner's Sons, 1985.

Gabbert, Lisa. "'Petting the Fabric': Medium and the Creative Process." *Uncoverings* 21 (2000): 137–53.

Gail, W. W., ed. *Yellowstone County Montana in the World War, 1917–1918–1919.* Billings, Mont.: War Book Publishing, 1919.

Gale, Mary E., and Margaret T. Ordoñez. "Eighteenth-century Indigo-resist Fabrics: Their Use in Quilts and Bed Hangings." *Uncoverings* 25 (2004): 157–79.

Gilbert, Jennifer. *The New England Quilt Museum Quilts: Featuring the Story of the Mill Girls, Instructions for Five Heirloom Quilts.* Lafayette, Calif.: C&T, 1999.

Gilbertson, Laurann. "Patterns of the New World: Quiltmaking among Norwegian Americans." *Uncoverings* 27 (2006): 157–96.

Glassie, Henry. "Meaningful Things and Appropriate Myths: The Artifact's Place in American Studies." In *Material Life in America, 1600–1860.* Edited by Robert Blair St. George, 63–92. Boston: Northeastern University Press, 1998.

Gunn, Virginia. "Crazy Quilts and Outline Quilts: Popular Responses to the Decorative Arts/Art Needlework Movement, 1876–1893." *Uncoverings* 5 (1984): 131–52.

———. "Quilts at Nineteenth Century State and County Fairs: An Ohio Study." *Uncoverings* 9 (1988): 105–28.

———. "Quilts for Civil War Soldiers from Peacham, Vermont." *Uncoverings* 22 (2001).

———. "Yo-Yo or Bed-of-Roses Quilts: Nineteenth Century Origins." *Uncoverings* 8 (1987): 129–46.

Haaglund, Lois Flansburg. *Tough, Willing, and Able: Tales of a Montana Family.* Missoula, Mont.: Mountain Press, 1997.

Hall, Carrie A., and Rose G. Kretsinger. *The Romance of the Patchwork Quilt in America.* 1935. Reprint, Caldwell, Idaho: Caxton, 1947.

Hall, Jane, and Dixie Haywood. *Foundation Quilts: Building on the Past.* Paducah, Ky.: American Quilter's Society, 2000.

Hamilton-Merritt, Jane. *Tragic Mountains: The Hmong, the Americans, and the Secret War for Laos, 1942–1992.* Bloomington: Indiana University Press, 1999.

Harber, Nora E., ed. *Our Fort Benton of Yesterday and Today.* Fort Benton, Mont.: River Press, n.d.

Harris, Alma, ed. *Quilts of Alaska: A Textile Album of the Last Frontier.* Juneau, Alaska: Gastineau Channel Historical Society, 2001.

Hawkins, Beverly. "A Generous Spirit." *Country Home*, June 1993, 82–86.

Hedges, Elaine. *Hearts and Hands: Women, Quilts, and American Society.* 1987. Reprint, Nashville, Tenn.: Rutledge Hill, 1996.

Heine, Laura. *Color Fusion.* Columbus, Ohio: DragonThreads, 2001.

Hemming, Jill. "Waccamaw-Siouan Quilts: A Model for Studying Native American Quilting." *Uncoverings* 18 (1997): 189–211.

Hoag, Alice Barnes, and Mrs. Matthew W. Alderson. *Historical Sketch of the Montana Woman's Christian Temperance Union, 1883–1912.* Helena, Mont.: State Publishing, 1912.

Holmes, Krys. *Montana: Stories of the Land.* Helena: Montana Historical Society Press, 2008.

Hood, Yolanda. "The Culture of Resistance: African American Art Quilts and Self-Defining." *Uncoverings* 22 (2001): 141–69.

Hopgood, Freddie. "Under 'Drunkard's Pathway.'" *Billings (Mont.) Gazette*, December 15, 1968.

Horton, Laurel, et al. *Quiltmaking in America: Beyond the Myths.* Nashville, Tenn.: Rutledge Hill, 1994.

Hurley, Mary, and Marian S. Sweeney. *Celebrating One Hundred Years: The Montana Centennial Quilt.* N.p., 1988.

Indiana Quilt Registry Project, Inc. *Quilts of Indiana: Crossroads of Memories.* Bloomington: Indiana University Press, 1991.

In the Years Gone By: Simpson, Cottonwood. Cottonwood, Mont.: Cottonwood Home Demonstration Club, 1964.

Jablonski, Ramona. *Folk Art Designs from Polish Wycinanki and Swiss and German Scherenschnitte.* Owings Mills, Md.: Stemmer House, 1978.

Jarrell, Mary Katherine. "Three Historic Quilts." *Uncoverings* 2 (1981): 97–104.

Jeffrey, Julie Roy. *Frontier Women: The Trans-Mississippi West, 1840–1880.* New York: Hill and Wang, 1979.

Jensen, Margaret, and Leila Williams. *Looking Back.* Denver: Big Mountain, 1966.

Kell, Katharine T. "Folk Names for Tobacco." *Journal of American Folklore* 79, no. 314 (1966): 590–99.

Kiracofe, Roderick. *The American Quilt: A History of Cloth and Comfort, 1750–1950.* New York: Clarkson Potter, 1993.

Kirkpatrick, Erma. "Quilts, Quiltmaking, and the *Progressive Farmer*: 1886–1935." *Uncoverings* 6 (1985): 137–45.

Klapper, Melissa. *Jewish Girls Coming of Age in America.* New York: New York University Press, 2005.

Knight, Joan. *Virginia Quilt Museum.* Charlottesville, Va.: Howell, 2002.

Kohl, Seena B. "'Well I have lived in Montana almost a week and like it fine': Letters from the Davis Homestead, 1910–1926." *Montana The Magazine of Western History* 51 (Autumn 2001): 40.

Lambert, Kirby, Patricia M. Burnham, and Susan R. Near. *Montana's State Capitol: The People's House.* Helena: Montana Historical Society Press, 2002.

Liles, James N. "Dyes in American Quilts Made Prior to 1930, with Special Emphasis on Cotton and Linen." *Uncoverings* 5 (1984): 29–40.

Loscalzo, Anita B. "The History of the Sewing Machine and Its Use in Quilting in the United States." *Uncoverings* 26 (2005): 175–208.

Lucey, Donna. *Photographing Montana, 1894–1928: The Life and Work of Evelyn Cameron.* New York: Knopf, 1990.

MacDowell, Marsha L., and C. Kurt Dewhurst, eds. *To Honor and Comfort: Native Quilting Traditions.* Santa Fe: Museum of New Mexico Press and Michigan State University Museum, 1997.

Mainardi, Patricia. "Quilts: The Great American Art." *Feminist Art Journal* 2 (Winter 1973): 1, 18–23.

Malarcher, Patricia. "Quilts: Folk Art to Fine Art in Newark." *New York Times*, March 22, 1987.

Malone, Michael P., Richard B. Roeder, and William L. Lang. *Montana: A History of Two Centuries.* Rev. ed. Seattle: University of Washington Press, 1991.

Marcus, Jacob Rader. *United States Jewry, 1776–1995.* Detroit: Wayne State University Press, 1989.

Marling, Karal Ann. *Blue Ribbon: A Social and Pictorial History of the Minnesota State Fair.* St. Paul: Minnesota Historical Society Press, 1990.

Mathews, Allan James. *A Guide to Historic Missoula.* Helena: Montana Historical Society Press, 2002.

McGeschick, Joe, David Miller, Jim Shanley, Caleb Shields, and Dennis Smith. *The History of the Assiniboine and Sioux Tribes of the Fort Peck Indian Reservation, Montana, 1800–2000.* Helena: Fort Peck Community College and Montana Historical Society Press, 2008.

McPherson, James. *Battle Cry of Freedom: The Civil War Era.* Oxford, U.K.: Oxford University Press, 1988.

Meyer, Suellen. "Early Influences of the Sewing Machine and Visible Machine Stitching on Nineteenth-century Quilts." *Uncoverings* 10 (1989): 38–53.

Milspaw, Yvonne J. "Regional Style in Quilt Design." *Journal of American Folklore* 110 (Autumn 1997): 363–90.

Minnesota Quilt Project. *Minnesota Quilts: Creating Connections with Our Past.* Stillwater, Minn.: Voyageur, 2005.

Murphy, Mary. *Hope in Hard Times: New Deal Photographs of Montana, 1936–1942.* Helena: Montana Historical Society Press, 2003.

Myers, Rex C., ed. *Lizzie: The Letters of Elizabeth Chester Fisk, 1864–189.* Missoula, Mont.: Mountain Press, 1989.

Nickols, Pat L. "The Use of Cotton Sacks in Quiltmaking." *Uncoverings* 9 (1988): 57–64.

O'Dowd, Karen. "Quilting in Big Sky Country." *Lady's Circle Patchwork Quilts*, January 1993, 6–11.

Olson, Jeanne Field. "Love in Every Stitch: Quilting in Montana." *Montana Magazine*, November–December 1996.

Ordoñez, Margaret T. "Ink Damage on Nineteenth Century Cotton Signature Quilts." *Uncoverings* 13 (1992): 148–68.

Orlofsky, Patsy, and Myron Orlofsky. *Quilts in America.* 1974. Reprint, New York: Abbeville Press, 1992.

Parker, Linda. *Montana Star Quilts.* Helena, Mont.: Montana Quilts, 1997.

Peaden, Joyce B. "Donated Quilts Warmed Wartorn Europe." *Uncoverings* 9 (1988): 29–44.

Pearce, T. M. "Three Rocky Mountain Terms: Park, Sugan, and Plaza." *American Speech* 33 (May 1958): 99–107.

Pease, Margery. *A Worthy Work in a Needy Time: The Montana Industrial School for Indians (Bond's Mission), 1886–1897.* N.p., 1986.

Peavy, Linda, and Ursula Smith. *The Gold Rush Widows of Little*

Falls: A Story Drawn from the Letters of Pamelia and James Fergus. St. Paul: Minnesota Historical Society Press, 1990.

Perry, Rosalind. A Joy Forever: Marie Webster's Quilt Patterns. Santa Barbara, Calif.: Practical Patchwork, 1992.

Przybysz, Jane. "Competing Cultural Values at the Great American Quilt Festival." Uncoverings 8 (1987): 107–27.

Pulford, Florence. Morning Star Quilts: A Presentation of the Work and Lives of Northern Plains Indian Women. Los Altos, Calif.: Leone, 1989.

Ramsey, Bets. "Art and Quilts: 1950–1970." Uncoverings 14 (1993): 9–40.

Ramsey, Bets, and Merikay Waldvogel. The Quilts of Tennessee: Images of Domestic Life Prior to 1930. Nashville, Tenn.: Rutledge Hill, 1986.

Rhoades, Ruth. "Feed Sacks in Georgia: Their Manufacture, Marketing, and Consumer Use." Uncoverings 18 (1997): 121–52.

Riley, Glenda. "American Daughters: Black Women in the West." Montana The Magazine of Western History 38 (Spring 1988): 14–27.

Ritch, Johnny. Horsefeathers. Helena, Mont.: Naegele Printing, 1940.

Roberson, Ruth Haislip, ed. North Carolina Quilts. Chapel Hill: University of North Carolina Press, 1988.

Ronan, Mary. Girl from the Gulches: The Story of Mary Ronan as Told to Margaret Ronan. Edited by Ellen Baumler. Helena: Montana Historical Society Press, 2003.

Rowley, Nancy J. "Red Cross Quilts for the Great War." Uncoverings 3 (1982): 43–51.

Schläpfer-Geiser, Susanne. Traditional Papercutting: The Art of Scherenschnitte. New York: Lark Books, 1997.

Schlereth, Thomas J. "Country Stores, County Fairs, and Mail-order Catalogues: Consumption in Rural America." In Consuming Visions: Accumulation and Display of Goods in America, 1880–1920. Edited by Simon J. Broner. New York: W.W. Norton, 1989.

Schmeal, Jacqueline Andre. Patchwork: Iowa Quilts and Quilters. Iowa City: University of Iowa Press, 2003.

Segars, Loretta. One Hundred Years in Culbertson, 1887–1987. N.p., 1986.

Senft, Carolyn. "Cultural Artifact and Architectural Form: A Museum of Quilts and Quilt Making." Journal of Architectural Education 48 (February 1995): 144–53.

Shaw, Robert. The Art Quilt. New York: Hugh Lauter Levin Associates, 1997.

Smith, Norma. Jeannette Rankin, America's Conscience. Helena: Montana Historical Society Press, 2002.

Smith, Wilene. "Quilt History in Old Periodicals." Uncoverings 11 (1990): 188–213.

Stolz, Mildred K. This Is Yours: The Montana Farmers Union and Its Cooperative Associates. Minneapolis: Lund, 1956.

Stonuey, Joseph F., and Patricia Cox Crews. "The Nebraska Quilt History Project: Interpretations of Selected Parameters." Uncoverings 9 (1988): 151–69.

Stout, Tom, ed. Montana, Its Story and Biography: A History of Aboriginal and Territorial Montana and Three Decades of Statehood. Vol. 2. Chicago: American Historical Society, 1921.

Sullivan, Kathlyn F. Gatherings: America's Quilt Heritage. Paducah, Ky.: American Quilter's Society, 1995.

Swan, Kenneth D. Splendid Was the Trail. Missoula, Mont.: Mountain Press, 1968.

Swaney, Alexandra, ed. From the Heart and Hand: Montana Folk and Traditional Arts Apprenticeships, 1992–1996. Helena, Mont.: Montana Folklife Program of the Montana Arts Council, 2001.

Taylor, Quintard. "The Emergence of Black Communities in the Pacific Northwest: 1865–1910." Journal of Negro History 64 (Autumn 1979): 342–54.

Taylor, Quintard, and Shirley Ann Wilson Moore, eds. African American Women Confront the West, 1600–2000. Norman: University of Oklahoma Press, 2003.

Termin, Shawn. To Honor and Comfort: Native American Quilting Traditions. Washington, D.C.: Smithsonian Institution/ National Museum of the American Indian, 1997.

Texas Heritage Quilt Society. Texas Quilts: Texas Treasures. Paducah, Ky.: American Quilter's Society, 1986.

Tobin, Jacqueline L., and Raymond G. Dobard. Hidden in Plain View: The Secret Story of Quilts and the Underground Railroad. New York: Doubleday, 1999.

Trestain, Eileen Jahnke. Dating Fabrics: A Color Guide, 1800–1960. Paducah, Ky.: American Quilter's Society, 1998.

Tucker, Nancy H. Indian Star Quilts: Women in Transition. Ware, Mass.: Mary S. & Niles Tucker, 1999.

Twelker, Nancyann Johnson. Women and Their Quilts: A Washington State Centennial Tribute. Bothell, Wash.: That Patchwork Place, 1988.

Ulrich, Laurel Thatcher. "Pens and Needles: Documents and Artifacts in Women's History." Uncoverings 14 (1993): 221–28.

Waldvogel, Merikay. "The Origin of Mountain Mist Patterns." Uncoverings 16 (1995): 95–137.

———. Soft Covers for Hard Times: Quiltmaking and the Great Depression. Nashville, Tenn.: Rutledge Hill, 1990.

Waldvogel, Merikay, and Barbara Brackman. Patchwork Souvenirs of the 1933 World's Fair: The Sears National Quilt Contest and Chicago's Century of Progress Exposition. Nashville, Tenn.: Rutledge Hill, 1993.

Webster, Marie D. Quilts: Their Story and How to Make Them. Garden City, N.Y.: Doubleday, Page, 1915.

Welter, Barbara. "The Cult of True Womanhood." American Quarterly 18, no. 2 (Summer 1966): 52.

Welters, Linda, and Margaret Ordoñez. "Early Calico Printing in Rhode Island." Uncoverings 22 (2001): 65–85.

Winestine, Belle Fligelman. "Mother Was Shocked." Montana The Magazine of Western History 24 (Summer 1974): 70–79.

Wolf, Helen Pease. Reaching Both Ways. Laramie, Wyo.: Jelm Mountain, 1989.

Woodward, Thomas K., and Blanche Greenstein. Crib Quilts and Other Small Wonders: Including Complete Patterns and Instructions for Making Your Own Crib Quilts. New York: E. P. Dutton, 1981.

———. Twentieth Century Quilts, 1900–1950. New York: E. P. Dutton, 1981.

Yesteryears and Pioneers: Wheatland County. Harlowton, Mont.: Harlowton Woman's Club, 1972.

Credits for quilts, graphics, and photographs reproduced in *Border to Border*

Frontispiece: Red and Green quilt, MHSM,
gift of Diana Foote Lawrence, DO
vi: Courtesy Shirley Barrett, Kalispell, JR
viii: Courtesy Eleanor Thorson, Kalispell, JR
xii: MHSM, gift of Kenneth Kohl, DO
xiv: Left courtesy C. Karen Stanton, Hardin;
center courtesy Gayle Shirley, Helena, Gayle
Shirley photo; right, *Bozeman Daily Chronicle*,
Deirdre Eitel photo
xv: Courtesy Myrtle P. Hubley, Billings
xvi: Modified Necktie, MHSM, gift of Jim
Franks, DO

2–3: MOR, donors Annabel Durnford and
Kathryn Cornue
4: Top courtesy Mary Murphy, Bozeman;
bottom *The 1902 Edition of the Sears Roebuck
Catalogue* (reprint; New York, 1969), 723
5: Left MHSPA, PAc 84-53; right MHSA, SC
1699
7: MHSPA, 949-936, R. H. McKay photo
8: MHSM, gift of Minnie Dissett Webb, DO
9: Courtesy Our Savior's Lutheran Church,
Box Elder
10: MHSPA, 955-531
11: AC 9002, copyright DMNS, Christina Jackson photo
12: Left MHSM, JR; upper right MHSPA, 981-
071; lower right © photograph by Michael
Crummett
13: MHSM, gift of Arthur William Schmidt
14: MHSPA, PAc 77-94 v.1, p.19.1
15: MHSM, gift of Bill Kitterman, DO
16: Top MHSM, gift of Mrs. J.H. Griswold, DO;
bottom MHSPA, PAc 83-55
17: Top detail, MHSM, gift of Ladies Auxiliary
to Council 349, DO; bottom MHSPA, PAc
96-47.2
18: Both SPL
19: Left MHSPA, 942-296; right MHSPA,
942-299
20: LC-USF 34-027515-D, Arthur Rothstein
photo
21: Courtesy Laura Howell and Edith Frey, JR
22, 24: Quilt detail and quilt, CFC, gift of Bill
Kitterman, DO
24: Top right, MHSPA, 955-110; lower right
MHSPA, lot 22, box 4, F17.1
25: Top Edward S. Curtis Collection,
LC-USZ62-66670, Edward S. Curtis photo;
center courtesy Carol Jo Thompson, Bozeman, W. F. Page photo
26: Top MHSPA, 942-167; bottom MHSPA,
PAc 74-72.1
27: Courtesy Jack and Susan Davis, Olde
America Antiques
28: Top left and top right, courtesy William
and Leslie Goss Family, JRs; center courtesy
Kati Williams, Hobson, JR
29: Courtesy Doris P. Weisner, Augusta, JR
30–31: All courtesy Maxine Otis Family,
Hobson, JRs
32–33: All courtesy Jane Davidson Klockman
Family, Bozeman, quilt and quilt detail JR
34–35: Courtesy Reva Parker, Bozeman, JR
36–37: Quilt and quilt detail courtesy Phyllis
Jewell, Fort Benton, JRs; cutout design from

Barbara Anne Townshend, *Introduction to the
Art of Cutting Groups of Figures, Flowers, Birds,
etc., in Black Paper* (London, 1815–16), n.p.
38–39: Courtesy Jean M. Kimble, Missoula, JR
40–41: Quilt courtesy Michelle Salisbury, JR;
sisters courtesy Virginia M. Fox, Fort Benton
42–43: Quilt courtesy Catherine Booth
Koteskey, Great Falls, JRs; right *In from the
Fields*, MHSM
44–45: Quilt courtesy Jane Davidson
Klockman Family, Bozeman, JRs;
music room (detail) MHSPA, PAc 95-39.33,
M. D. Boland photo
46: Quilt courtesy Sue Lepley, Fort Benton, JR
47: Quilt MHSM, DO; Batchelders, courtesy
Sue Lepley, Fort Benton
48–49: Quilt courtesy Linda Gerrity Fagen-
strom, Great Falls, JRs
50–51: Both courtesy Maridona Fisher Norick,
Kalispell, quilt JR
52–53: Both courtesy Shirley Lindell, quilt JR
54: Courtesy Maria B. Winslow, Great Falls, JR
55: Quilt MHSM, gift of Susan Halley, DO;
detail from page 54 quilt
56–57: Both courtesy William Gillespie,
Radersburg, JRs
58–59: MHSM, CFC, gift of Bill Kitterman, quilt
DO, detail JR
60–61: Quilt courtesy Beth Smith Duke,
Great Falls, JR; ad courtesy Jack and Susan
Davis, Olde America Antiques
62–63: All courtesy great-granddaughter Anna
Owens, Missoula, quilts JRs
64–65: Quilt courtesy Edith G. Torske,
Hardin, JR; steamboat MHSPA, H-317, F. Jay
Haynes, photographer, Haynes Foundation
Collection
66–67: Quilt and bottom right courtesy
Charlotte (Quigley) Orr and the James
Fergus Family, Lewistown, JR; right top
MHSPA, 942-157, Reiman and Company
photo
68: MHSM, gift of Gladys Hardin, DO
70: Top MHSPA, 954-187; center MHSPA,
PAc 99-29
71: MHSPA, left PAc 90-87.4-3, right PAc 90-
87.68-1, both Evelyn Cameron photos
72: Top left from *Montgomery Ward & Co.
Catalogue and Buyers' Guide* (1895; reprint,
New York, 1969), 263; top right and bottom
left courtesy Jack and Susan Davis, Olde
America Antiques
73: Top (detail) WHC, gift of Mrs. Charles (Virginia) Marvin Family, JR; bottom left cour-

tesy Myrtle P. Hubley, Billings, JR; bottom right courtesy Shirley Barrett, Kalispell, JR

74–75: Quilt MHSM, gift of Frieda Fligelman and Belle Fligelman Winestine, JR; top right MHSPA, PAc 87-103 F1, Rugg photo; bottom right MHSPA, 953-216

76–77: Courtesy Frances M. Wyler, Great Falls, quilt JR

78–79: MHSM, gift of Mrs. Oscia MacGinniss, JRs

80–91: Quilt detail left HMFM, Leona Roberson Collection, 1987.31.1, JR; quilt detail right MHSM, gift of Jim Franks, DO

82–83 All courtesy Jan Swartz, quilt and sham JRs

84–85: Quilt MHSM, gift of Karen Jenson & Reginald Rutherford III, quilt detail DO, quilt JR; married officers' quarters MHSPA, 946-932

86–87: Quilt MHSM, gift of Doreen Cook, JR; Blackfoot City PCMAF

88–89: Quilt courtesy Doris A. Schledorn, Bozeman, JR; wagons MOR, C. O. Corey photo

90–91: All courtesy Robert and Alice Ford, Kalispell, quilt JR, Ford family, B. L. Beaman photo

92–93: Quilt and Bennetts courtesy Marshall and Luzann Bennett, Bozeman, quilt JR; Scofield and Ames from Range Rider Reps, *Fanning the Embers* (Miles City, Mont., 1971), 5

94–95: Quilt courtesy Lucille Lussenden, Choteau, JR; family courtesy Karen Lussenden McNutt, Sidney

96–97: All courtesy of those warmed by Edna Mae Miller's love, Big Horn, quilt JR

98–99: Quilt left and detail center E. C. Baxter Family (Mary Law Mollander), JR

99: Top right courtesy Baxter Family Archives; bottom right courtesy G. D. Martin Family, Two Dot, JR

100–101: Quilt courtesy Wegener Family, Whitehall, JR; Mayflower Mine Jefferson Valley Museum, Whitehall

102–103: Quilt MHSM, DO, Red Cross volunteers, MHSPA, PAc 96-47

104–105: Quilt CMM, gift of Sigrid and Orvin Fjare, quilt JR; Red Cross parade from W. W. Gail, ed., *Yellowstone County Montana in the World War, 1917–1919* (Billings, Montana, 1919)

106–107: All Heritage Committee, First Presbyterian Church, Missoula, quilt JR, church R. H. McKay photo

108–109: Quilt courtesy William L. Sanguine, Kalispell, and H. Earl Clack Museum, Havre, JR; family courtesy William L. Sanguine, Kalispell

110: MHSM, gift of Susan Near, DO

112: Top MHSPA, PAc 77-94 I.46.2, Henry B. Syverud, photo; bottom MHSPA Fort Peck Dam Collection

113: Top MSU, Olga Ross Hannon photo, from William E. Farr, *The Reservation Blackfeet, 1882–1945: A Photographic History of Cultural Survival* (Seattle, 1984), 134; bottom MHSPA, PAc 89-38.13, A. E. Wartena photo

114: MHSM, gift of Marcia Vollmer, DO

115: Top left courtesy Jack and Susan Davis, Olde America Antiques; top right and center MHSM, gift of Linda O'Connell, DO

116–117: Quilt left courtesy Libby DuBois Pettit, Missoula, JR; top right MHSM, gift of Lucille W. Thompson, JR; bottom right MHSPA, PAc 96-25.1

118–119: Quilt courtesy Barbara Baird Varner Hauge in memory of our Farmers Union Pioneers, JR; bottom center from Mildred K. Stoltz, *This Is Yours: The Montana Farmers Union and Its Cooperative Associates* (Minneapolis, 1956), following p. 98; lower right courtesy Barbara Hauge, Turner

120–121: Quilt left courtesy Doris Ann Stephens Pascal, Great Falls, JR; quilt center courtesy Irma Torske and Karen Torske Stanton, Hardin; top and bottom right courtesy Doris Ann Stephens Pascal, Great Falls

122–123: Quilt courtesy Byron and Mabel O'Neil Family, Kalispell, JR; family courtesy Robert O'Neil, Kalispell

124–125: Quilt courtesy Richard J. Weisner Family, JR; center and right courtesy Doris P. Weisner

126–127: All courtesy Nancy D. Marks, Townsend, quilts JRs

128–129: Quilts courtesy Marjorie Miner Solberg, JRs; right top and center courtesy Gaylord Miner, Ossette

130–131: All courtesy Cecelia Goodman, Bozeman, quilt JRs

132–133: All courtesy Laura Howell and Marjorie Arneson, Billings, quilt JRs

134–135: Both courtesy Fred Waylett Family, Missoula, quilt JR

136–137: Quilt and portrait courtesy Marshall and Luzann Bennett, Bozeman, quilt JR; bottom right from Frederick Herrschner, Inc., *Art Needlework and Fancy Wear for Women and Children* (Chicago, 1929), 22

138–139: Quilts courtesy Wilda May O'Neil Wilson Family, Kalispell, JRs; portrait courtesy Barbara "Bobbie" Truckner, Kalispell

140–141: All courtesy Edith Degner Duty, Billings, quilt JR

142–143: All courtesy Hilda Snapp Family, Lewistown, quilt JRs

144–145: All courtesy Kathie Sybrant, Great Falls, quilt JR

146: MHSM, gift of Grace Probert, DO

148: Top WPA Poster Collection, Prints and Photographs Division, LC-USZC2-5382; bottom MAFB

149: Top PM; bottom MHSPA, PAc 88-18.4

150–151: Quilt courtesy Edith Howell Frey and Marjorie Arneson, JRs; top left courtesy Marjorie Arneson, Billings

152–153: Quilt courtesy Edith Howell Frey, JRs; top right courtesy Marjorie Arneson, Billings

154–155: Both BHCM

156–157: Quilt courtesy Leila Williams, Great Falls, JRs; top right from Margaret Jensen (assisted by Leila Williams), *Looking Back* (Denver, 1966), frontispiece

158–159: Quilt BHCM, JR; top right from registration form MHQP 22-00-36, MHSA

160–161: Quilt Irene Evers Collection, 1989.7.2, HMFM, JRs; top right Photo Album Acc 1999-28, Irene Evers Collection, UM

162–163: Quilt courtesy Mary Ruth Hammett and Family, St. Xavier, JR; top and bottom right from Helen Pease Wolf, *Reaching Both Ways* (Laramie, Wyo., 1989), 38, 116

164–165: Quilt and portrait courtesy Mick Stevens Family, Lodge Grass, quilt JR; right bottom DU

166–167: All courtesy Mary Wallace, Kalispell, quilt JRs

168–169: All MMHH, quilt and quilt detail JRs

170–171: All courtesy Cathryn Dyrdahl York, quilt JR

172–173: All courtesy Phyllis Jewell, Fort Benton, quilt JRs

174: MHSM, DO

176: Courtesy Suzanne Huston, Havre, JR

177: Courtesy of the Forrest Kitto Family, Toston, JR

178: Top left and right courtesy Susan Davis, Bozeman, quilt JR; bottom courtesy Phil Bell, photographer, Billings

179: Reprinted with permission of the *Billings Gazette*, Larry Mayer photo

180–181: All courtesy Myrna Miller Aamold, Benchland, quilt JRs

182–183: Quilts courtesy Mabel Lucas Family, JRs; top right courtesy Andrea Melton, Denton

184–185: All courtesy Elaine Graber, Kalispell, quilt JRs

186–187: MHSM, quilt JR, quilt detail, DO

188–189: All courtesy Shirley M. Barrett, Lakeside, quilt JRs

190–191: Both courtesy Charles and Shirley Rorvik, Kalispell, quilt JR

192–193: Quilt left courtesy Falls Quilt Guild, Great Falls, JR; quilt center MHSM, DO; top right courtesy Penny Rubner, Great Falls

194–195: Quilt courtesy Christian Jette, Billings, and Carolyn Jette, Stanford, JR; top right *Independent Record*, Helena, photo by George Lane, Brockton; bottom center *The Herald-News*, Wolf Point

196–197: Both courtesy Joan P. Hodgeboom, Quilt Gallery, Kalispell, quilt JR

198–199: Quilt courtesy Frances S. "Scottie" Byerly, PhD, JR; top right courtesy Shelly Van Haur, Hilger

200–201: Courtesy Kristi Billmayer, Havre, with permission of quilt pattern designer Karen K. Stone, JR; top right courtesy Kristi Billmayer, Hugh Dresser photo; quilt center MHSM, gift of Jane Addy, DO

202–203: Accession # 00.01.07, MMAC, donated by Helen Cappadocia

204–205: All courtesy the artist Libby DuBois Pettit, Missoula, quilt JRs; top right Stacy Davis photo

206–207: Quilt courtesy Betsi Pollington, Havre, JRs; top right courtesy Suzanne Huston, Havre; bottom right MHSPA, PAc 90-87 35-5, Evelyn Cameron photo

Index